PAUSE BREATHE GRATEFUL

TIMELESS TALES OF THANKFULNESS

AMARNATH SANKAR

Printed in India

IndiePress

ISBN: 978-93-6045-417-3

First Printing, 2025

IndiePress

A division of Nasadiya Technologies Private Ltd.

Koramangala, Bengaluru

Karnataka-560029

http://indiepress.in/

Edited by Anagha Somanakoppa

Typeset by MAP Systems, Bengaluru

Book Cover designed by Harsha Varthan

Publishing Consultant: Zoheb Ahmed

Author's Note

Dear Reader,

In this world of constant distractions and lost ability to focus on things, with a growing and alarming impact on mental health and well-being, I strongly believe that the practice of Pausing, Breathing, and being Grateful is a simple yet powerful way for you to align with your consciousness and regain the lost profoundness of your living experience that you truly deserve.

Welcome to "Pause, Breathe, Grateful!" a book that emerged from my transformative journey through the #365daysofGratitude project. This endeavor began as a personal commitment to recognize and record one thing I was grateful for every day for a year. This daily practice blossomed into a profound exploration that reshaped the way I look at life and the world!

Each day, I dedicated moments to pause, breathe, and reflect on the gifts life offered, whether it was an unexpected kindness, a moment of calm in a busy day, or a lesson from a challenging experience. This conscious process of noticing and appreciating the small (Or often unnoticed) things significantly deepened my connection to the world and the people around me, infusing each moment I live with a newfound sense of joy and contentment.

As the year progressed, the outcomes of this process became deeply ingrained in my being, turning gratitude from a fleeting feeling into a fundamental character trait.

Through "Pause Breathe Grateful," I share 100 selected stories/notes from this journey, hoping to inspire you to look within and around yourself and your life with an authentic sense of gratefulness. My wish is that these stories/notes may inspire you to start your own gratitude practice regime, discovering the transformative power of taking a moment to pause, breathe, and be grateful.

With Gratitude,

Amarnath Sankar

How to Use This Book/ Tool Effectively

The way you engage with "Pause, Breathe, Grateful" is completely up to you. This book is designed to fit seamlessly into your daily life, allowing you to explore gratitude at your own pace. With 100 chapters, each correlating to distinct moments of gratitude, you might choose to read one chapter each morning or before bed. After reading, Pause for a while, Breathe, and take a moment to sit in silence, absorbing the perspectives shared. Reflect on their meaning in your life and feel Grateful.

To deepen your sense of gratefulness, consider using the next two or three days to reflect further on what you've read. You can jot down your thoughts, feelings, and any insights that arise in a personal journal. This process of writing can enhance your perception and appreciation of each experience.

You'll find the "Self Reflection Prompts" section at the end of the book. This part offers a specific question for each chapter, designed to enhance your perception through introspection. It can serve as a valuable tool if you're seeking additional guidance or a starting point for deeper reflection.

"Pause, Breathe, Grateful" is more than just a book; it's a tool to help you nurture a practice of gratitude through mindfulness. Whether you engage with the self-reflection prompts provided or embark on your own reflective journey, each story is an invitation to recognize and cherish the abundance of life's blessings.

Contents

1. The Tale Of The SRK Of Jaipur 1

2. Synaptic Symphony:
   The Orchestra Of Life 3

3. Pale Blue Dot: Cosmic Perspective 5

4. Gutenberg's Legacy:
   The Printing Revolution Reimagined 7

5. Water: The New Gold 9

6. Half-Hearted Encore:
   Lessons From The Stage 11

7. Unleashing Strengths:
   Insights From The Iliad 15

8. A Productive Tip From The Interview 17

9. Victory From Within: Sun Tzu's
   Winning Attitude 21

10. The Blue And Red Letters 23

11. A Reflection On Raman Naik's Story 25

12. Nobody Was Ever Thinking About You 29

13. The Eternal Breath: A Grateful Reflection 31

14. Forgiveness: A Divine Path 33

15. Home: A Sheltering Reminder 35

16. Silent Blossoms: Unsung Heroes Of Cleanliness 37

17. Unbreakable Spirit: Lessons From Louis Zamperini 39

18. Candles That Illuminate The Lives Of Others 41

19. Echoes Of Yesterday: Embracing The Sum Of Our Past 43

20. The Legacy Of Sir Nicholas Winton 45

21. Travel That Unlocks Change 47

22. Diversify Your Investments: Eggs And Baskets 49

23. Surrender: Guiding You Through Unknown Chapters 51

24. Inspiration Everywhere: Finding Motivation In The World Around Us 53

25. Rich Dad Poor Dad 55

26. True Richness: Beyond The Illusion Of Wealth 57

27. The Temple Of The Heart 59

28. The Mystery Of 'Empty Eye' 61

29. No Half Measures, Period 63

30. An Unforgettable Meal From An Angel In The Skies 65

31. Be Intentionally Deaf When You Move Forward 69

32. Simply Vanilla 71

33. Fashion Model 73

34. A Spoonful Of Kindness: A Sweet Childhood Memory 75

35. A Gamble Wheel On The Question Paper 77

36. Being In The Flow Of Life 81

37. Curiosity And The Rewarding Circuit In The Brain 83
38. Understanding Loss Aversion 85
39. Sailing 87
40. Rasam: The Magical Recipe 89
41. Unlove: A Liberation From Limiting Love 91
42. Matrix Defines Purpose 93
43. Attitude Of Being A Custodian 95
44. When Emojis Disrupted The Way We Communicate 97
45. Guru Dispels The Darkness Of Ignorance 99
46. We Can Wait A Minute 101
47. Legend Of Field Marshal Sam Manekshaw 103
48. Goddess Of Grace: A Teacher's Gift On Onam 107
49. Niyyah: The Purpose Behind Every Action 109
50. Musa The Trillionaire: Emperor Of The Salt 111
51. The Power Of Undivided Attention 113

52. Parallel Tracks Of Influence:
Balancing Forces In History 115
53. Tamil: Language Of The Heart 117
54. Beyond The Physical:
Exploring Receptivity 121
55. Inclusive Innovation:
Lessons From Hong Kong 123
56. Kuyili: The Immortal Warrior of Sivaganga 125
57. Embracing The Subtle Extraordinary 127
58. Humans Of Tokyo 129
59. A Sustainable Footwear Revolution..................133
60. Sculpting Minimalism:
Crafting Beauty In Simplicity............................135
61. The Empty Pot: A Seeker's Perspective 137
62. Shades Of Blue: Comfort And Joy....................139
63. The Dance Of Meaningful Coincidences 141
64. Mondo Bongo 143
65. You Can Touch The Way 'Deeper' 145

66. Choosing The Five:
The Power Of Social Circles 147

67. Wabi-Sabi: Embracing
Imperfect Perfection 149

68. Exascale Computing: Revolutionizing Our
Technological Landscape 151

69. It's Not Net Sitting Or Net Eating 153

70. Sowing Seeds Of Patience:
Lessons From The Farmland 155

71. Timenomics: Maximizing
The Value Of Every Second 157

72. Dots: Simplifying Success,
One Hour At A Time 159

73. Cracking The Habit Loop:
Insights From The Power Of Habit 161

74. Gut Microbiome: Guardians
Of Our Well-Being 163

75. Tonality: Enhancing
Communication Effectiveness 165

76. Spreading Smiles 167

77. Transforming Should Be Into Musts 169

78. Memories Framed:
Gratitude For Photographs.....171

79. An Angel On The Highway.....173

80. Discerning Love: What It Is And Isn't.....175

81. Leadership In Adversity:
Embracing Failure With Responsibility.....177

82. Heartfelt Correction:
A Grateful Remembrance.....181

83. Seeds Of Devil And Divine.....185

84. Guarding Dignity: Stories
Behind The Uniform.....187

85. A Cosmic Response.....191

86. The Journey Vs. Destination.....195

87. For All Unknown Singers.....197

88. The Art Of Introspection.....199

89. The Power Of Follow-Up.....201

90. Kindness Brewed With Tea.....203

91. Tale Of Sudhakaran: The Luckseller.....205

92. Decisive Whispers:
Your Body's Guidance.....207

93. The Procrastination Puzzle: Unraveling Its Psychology 209

94. Mocha: A Journey From Port To Palate 211

95. Transistors: The Invisible Architects Of The Digital Age 213

96. The Witness State: Navigating Life's Unfolding Journey..................................215

97. Night Owl Reflections 217

98. Only This Will Lead You To That 219

99. When They Go Low, We Go High................221

100. The Power Of Gratitude 223

SELF-REFLECTION PROMPTS.........................225

Dedication + Flashback 277

About the Author...279

Connect with the Author 281

1.

The Tale Of The SRK Of Jaipur

I was in Jaipur last year, and at a shop in Johri Bazaar, I met a vibrant, charming, handsome guy, someone who looked exactly like a Shah Rukh Khan character - his mannerisms, clothes, hairstyle.

His unbelievable salesmanship made me buy much more than I had intended to. I thought that the owner of the shop was blessed to have such a salesman. We know how hard it is to close a sale, it's a beautiful art.

When the point of negotiation came, I tried to communicate with him, but he was unable to understand what I said since my Hindi was not good enough. Finally, I used the Google Translator app to translate from English to Hindi and showed him the text. His face immediately paled. His eyes showed fear and sorrow, and I wondered if I had done something wrong. I had no clue what had made him so deflated.

I went to the shop owner and told him, "I just showed this to the sales guy, and it made him very sad. I just wanted to negotiate." The owner smiled and told me, "Sir, it's because he is unable to read and write; he is illiterate."

I could not imagine that in 21st-century India, a 20-something boy, a vibrant salesman at Johri Bazaar, could not read and write. I left after I made my purchases, but the whole night, I was thinking about my Shah Rukh Khan of Jaipur.

When I look back, I am grateful for my ability to read and write, and I hope when you are reading this, you, too, realize the value of literacy!

* * *

2.

Synaptic Symphony: The Orchestra Of Life

A fundamental factor in our body that brings us the experience of living is our 'Neurons.' Whatever we think, do, experience -- it is all controlled and made possible through them.

Neurons are known to everybody, and recently, I happened to discuss with a senior at my school who has been doing deep research on them.

He shared an insight about synapses, which are the tiny communication links between neurons. On average, the human brain has 100 billion neurons, and each neuron is connected to 1000 to 10,000 synapses. There are about 100 to 1000 trillion synapses in our brain alone.

Each synapse is like a tiny computer. It can load and run different programs and change and adapt in response to different firing patterns. Synapses help us learn and remember.

These tiny little communication links enable almost every experience we have on this planet, including the sense of bliss, hunger, confusion, anger, and love.

Constant electrochemical reactions and exchanges make us and our system alive. Although I was aware of neurons in general, I found the communication links that are the synapses and their role quite interesting.

I think we should extend our gratitude to these synapses that are not even visible to our eyes, but make the experience of life on this planet possible.

* * *

3.

Pale Blue Dot: Cosmic Perspective

Voyager 1 was a space probe launched by NASA in 1977. In 1990, when it was about 6 billion kilometers away from Earth, it captured a photograph of our planet from interstellar space. In the vast cosmos, Earth appeared as just a tiny dot.

The astronomer Carl Sagan wrote a book titled Pale Blue Dot inspired by this photograph taken by Voyager 1. Sagan remarked that "Astronomy is a humbling and character-building experience. There is perhaps no better demonstration of the folly of human conceits than this distant image of our tiny world. To me, it underscores our responsibility to deal more kindly with one another and to preserve and cherish the pale blue dot, the only home we've ever known."

In our lives, we experience joy and suffering, countless religions, conflicting ideologies, and economic doctrines. Every hero, coward, creator, and destroyer of civilization, king and peasant—everyone who has ever lived—has lived on Earth. Yet, in the vast cosmic arena, Earth is just a pale blue dot, which is truly a humbling perspective.

As individuals, societies, nations, or even on a global scale, our lives and affairs seem significant. People worry and think about these matters as if they are solid, everlasting, and of great importance to the universe. But ultimately, even all of Earth is just a tiny speck, a dot-like dust particle in the vastness of the universe. When we look at ourselves from that broad perspective, life becomes a very simple matter, a very simple happening altogether.

It's a wonderful perspective to take things lightly and have a smooth and beautiful life ahead.

On this first day of 2021, I am grateful to share Carl Sagan's perspective with you.

* * *

4.

Gutenberg's Legacy: The Printing Revolution Reimagined

I recently had a discussion with a friend who published a book on Amazon that became a bestseller in certain online categories. He is one of the most voracious readers in my friend circle and was so excited to talk about the printing and publishing revolution taking place over the last ten years. He highlighted how difficult it used to be for an individual to publish a book and how technology and independent publishers have now disrupted the traditional processes.

After the conversation, I thought of Johannes Gutenberg, whom we learned about in school as the inventor of mechanical printing technology. His work kicked off the printing revolution in the world about

600 years ago. Gutenberg's invention played a key role in the development of the Renaissance, the Scientific Revolution, and consequently, the modern knowledge-based economy and the spread of learning to the masses.

All these changes were sparked by a goldsmith's wild idea, which led to the emergence of countless readers and writers. We are now living in the 21st century, witnessing another leap in innovation that has the power to influence empires and redefine the power dynamics of entertainment and civilization.

Today, I gratefully remember Gutenberg for his incredible innovation.

* * *

5.

Water: The New Gold

I read in the news one day that Wall Street is preparing to trade consumable water, which means water is officially joining the ranks of gold, oil, and other traded commodities. If this happens, it will allow water users to balance supply and demand more effectively.

According to the United Nations report, about 5 billion people will be affected by the shortage of consumable water across the world by 2050, making water the 'new oil.' I consider myself fortunate to have been born in a part of the world with abundant water resources where having a private well for homes is a common luxury. This contrasts starkly with the daily struggles faced by those who must work hard to access consumable freshwater.

Water is the basic, fundamental enabler of life, comprising nearly 80% of our bodies. In all our space explorations, we search for water to determine the possibility of life. Water is everything; water is life itself. Today, as we all drink fresh, usable water, let's be grateful and mindful of our consumption, considering our fellow beings and the entire ecosystem of our planet.

* * *

6.

Half-Hearted Encore: Lessons From The Stage

This happened when I was in high school or secondary school. We were instructed by the English department to create and perform a drama. I was the leader of one of the groups, adapted a story, and wrote a script for a drama that I directed. We had practiced thoroughly. I felt that other groups weren't as serious, but my group had really learned the script well and rehearsed in the evenings. On the day of our performance, we surprisingly did well in front of our friends and teachers.

I played the protagonist and had a clear vision of how to perform. This experience revealed a new dimension of my abilities to my friends. I was quite satisfied and was proud of both myself and the team. We received great appreciation from the students and teachers; we just stole the whole show!

After a couple of hours, some teachers who were not present in the morning heard about our performance and were eager to watch it. They approached us to perform it again! Personally, I was 100% against the idea. I couldn't imagine performing the same play to almost the same audience in the same place again on the same day.

I knew I couldn't replicate what had happened earlier. The performance wasn't repeatable because many of the good moments on stage were spontaneous. I lacked confidence and interest in repeating it. However, we were under great pressure from the teachers, and I wasn't strong enough to say no. My team members also thought they could do it again since they had already done it once.

The second time around, I was literally half-hearted, and it was a disaster! I had no personal interest in it and barely managed to deliver the dialogue, relying solely on my memory of the lines. There was no real performance; all I wanted was to wrap up the show and leave. Friends who had praised our morning performance watched us in the afternoon and remarked, "What a pathetic performance this is."

It was unusual–We had given our best and worst performances on the same day, on the same stage! The lesson I learned for a lifetime was: "Do not do anything half-heartedly. If you do, it will be devastating. On the other hand, if you do something wholeheartedly, even if you fail, you can take responsibility for the failure. But when you don't, you can't even take responsibility because you did it half-heartedly to begin with."

Today, I am gratefully remembering this unusual experience of a lifetime!

* * *

7.

Unleashing Strengths: Insights From The Iliad

Homer's *Iliad* describes the Trojan War, focusing on the Greek forces led by King Agamemnon and the greatest warrior, Achilles. Nestor, another Greek king and advisor to Agamemnon, engages in a conversation with him about Achilles as the war is about to start.

Agamemnon says to Nestor, "That man (Achilles) cannot be controlled; he doesn't listen to me."

Nestor pauses and then replies, "Achilles is a man born to end lives! You don't need to control him; you need to unleash him."

This is one of the finest quotes I have read in the *Iliad.* Achilles, the "killing machine," is one of the Greek army's greatest assets. However, Agamemnon has always been doubtful about Achilles' loyalty to his kingdom. Nestor advises Agamemnon to keep Achilles in the army, emphasizing that Achilles' ability to defeat enemies and win battles is a core strength and a core competency crucial for the Greek army's success against Troy.

This perspective is profound. When we reflect on ourselves, we recognize certain abilities as our core competencies. Sometimes, people, society, or other external factors may urge us to suppress these fundamental powers or instincts. However, it is these inborn talents that define who we truly are.

If you want to win the battle of life, you don't need to control your core strengths; you need to unleash them.

Today, I am extending my gratitude to Homer for the invaluable perspectives he has shared with humanity through his epics.

* * *

8.

A Productive Tip From The Interview

This happened during my last semester of engineering in college. I visited a friend who lived nearby and noticed he was dressed in executive-style attire, well-groomed, and sitting near his table in his room. His mobile phone was on the table, and he seemed to be waiting for something.

I asked, "Dude, it's study leave; we don't have class. Why are you in formals, and what are you doing here?" He replied, "Bro, I have an interview today."

I asked, "Where in Madurai?"

He said, "No, bro, it's a telephonic interview."

I laughed and said, "You fool, why are you dressed like this for a telephonic interview? Just pick up the call and speak; nobody is going to see you."

I made fun of him. He didn't respond with his usual banter or tell me why he chose to wear that attire. Normally, he would quarrel with me or joke back, but he stayed silent. As I left the room, I noticed a look in his eyes that seemed to say, "Man, I'm doing something right," but I just ignored it.

Nine years later, during the COVID-19 lockdown, I watched a video featuring a professor from Stanford University discussing how to be more productive while working from home. The number one tip he gave was, "Create a mental image, a sense of professionalism, by wearing the same attire you wear in the office." The professor explained that dressing in formal attire and applying the same perfume as you would for the office helps signal to your subconscious mind that you are ready to work, creating an environment that psychologically boosts productivity.

Hearing this, my mind flew back nine years! Some people have strong convictions like that; we may initially think it's foolish, but there's a certain magic in them that we may only recognize after many years.

This was a great lesson for me, and today, I am gratefully remembering that friend who dressed formally for a telephonic interview in his hostel room.

* * *

9.

Victory From Within: Sun Tzu's Winning Attitude

About eight years ago, an entrepreneur friend of mine introduced me to "The Art of War" by Sun Tzu. The Chinese General Sun Tzu is considered as one of the greatest military strategists, akin to Chanakya in India. "The Art of War" has always been one of my favorite books, and I want to share one of Sun Tzu's powerful perspectives here.

He said, "Victorious warriors win first and then go to war, while defeated warriors go to war first and then seek to win."

It's all about having a winning attitude. The message is simple: you must first win in your heart before you can win on the battlefield.

There are many perspectives from Sun Tzu that I'd like to share, but today I am gratefully remembering my friend who introduced me to "The Art of War."

* * *

10.

The Blue And Red Letters

This story is set in Germany during the time of fascist rule. People were afraid to communicate openly about their situation and the troubles they faced due to government censorship. All communication was monitored.

Two close friends living in different cities wanted to keep each other updated. They decided to write letters and figured out a way to secretly communicate their true feelings: whatever they wrote in blue ink would be the truth, and whatever they wrote in red ink would be false.

They waited weeks to receive each other's letters but managed to keep in touch. At one point, one of the friends went a long time without sending a letter. After many months, a letter arrived from him. It was on a beautiful cover, written entirely in blue ink, meaning that all of it was the truth.

In his letter, he said that the authorities had changed, becoming more humane. There were many infrastructural developments, ample food and supplies, no fights, peace everywhere, and the city was prosperous–it was heaven on earth. The friend who read the letter was excited and considered leaving his own city to join his friend.

As he read the letter line by line with great anticipation, he reached the end, where his friend explained that despite all the prosperity, abundance, and riches, there was one thing missing. He had searched everywhere but couldn't find it in the city: "There is no red ink available in the city to fill the pen; that is the only misery I am facing in the city." The letter ended there.

I truly believe that we are living in the freest world in recorded history. We might have underestimated the freedoms we experience, so today, let's be thankful for the freedoms we have.

* * *

11.

A Reflection On Raman Naik's Story

I travel a lot for work, and usually, if I feel comfortable at a particular hotel in a city, I try to stay there again. So, in every city and hotel I visit, I am quite familiar with the managers, waiters, room attendants, and staff.

There's a hotel in Gurgaon where a room attendant named Raman Naik assists me during the check-in process, provides room service, and so on if I need something from the pantry. I often ask people like him how much they earn and if they are able to survive on their salary. Raman told me that the hotel provides him with food and accommodation, and whatever he earns as a salary, he is able to send home to support his family. "It's a wonderful job," he told me.

One day, I arrived at the hotel quite late, hadn't had my dinner, and was hungry. I ordered food, and when it arrived, it was too much, enough for two or three people to have a full meal. I ate a little and placed the leftovers outside my room door. I was planning to go to sleep but felt very thirsty and needed a bottle of water. Not wanting to disturb Raman again, I went directly to the pantry. When I got there, I noticed that Raman was eating the leftovers I had placed outside my room.

He asked me, "Sir, how can I help you?"

I told him that I wanted water, and he gave me a couple of bottles.

I said, "Raman, you told me the hotel provides you with food."

He replied, "In this hotel, many customers don't finish the food they are served, especially during dinner time, so the management has given us permission to take the leftovers if we like."

When he said this, I didn't have much to say in response, so I just took the bottles and went back to my room.

This experience left me disturbed for many days and made me realize I have so much to be thankful for. Today, I'm expressing my gratitude for each meal I have eaten.

* * *

12.

Nobody Was Ever Thinking About You

For many people, when considering taking uncommon initiatives in life, the greatest fear that holds them back is the thought of how others might perceive their actions or moves.

In this context, I happened to read an excerpt from Elizabeth Gilbert's book *Big Magic.* In that book, there is a chapter titled "Nobody's Thinking About You." It's a beautiful chapter that explains how we often craft our lives based on the perspectives of others and society, particularly in our twenties and thirties. However, it is only when we reach our fifties or even sixties that we realize that nobody was ever truly thinking about us.

Most of the time, people are preoccupied with their own dreams, challenges, and problems. People's attention may be momentarily drawn to us when we make an uncommon move, but that attention does not last long. They might observe us, comment on our actions, and then move on because they have their own lives to manage.

Elizabeth Gilbert shares this perspective based on a discussion she had with a 70-year-old woman she met during her travels.

I personally feel this is a wonderful perspective. There is no need to be bothered by people in the gallery; play the game with total spirit and enjoy it to the fullest, following your own style of gameplay.

Today, I am gratefully remembering Elizabeth Gilbert and her book, *Big Magic.*

* * *

13.

The Eternal Breath: A Grateful Reflection

Today, I am gratefully reflecting on my breath. Most of us, including myself, take it for granted; we don't actually pay enough attention or give consideration to our breathing. But, ultimately, our breath is the most significant cause and the pillar of our existence. If we look at our lives, they are just a series of events that occur between two breaths: from the first breath we take when we come out of our mother's womb until the last breath we take before saying farewell to the planet.

Many things, people, and experiences may come and go within a lifetime, but breath is what stays with us from the day we open our eyes until the day we close them forever. At this very moment, there are thousands of human beings who have just taken their first breath and many thousands of others who have taken their last breath on this planet.

I am breathing as I write this, and you are breathing as you read it. So, let's take a deep breath and experience the life energy entering and filling us. Let's be conscious and aware of our breath, and in this moment, let's gratefully acknowledge and embrace the most important phenomenon of our lives!

* * *

14.

Forgiveness: A Divine Path

The state of being ready or emotionally evolved enough to ask for forgiveness or to give it–that is what I am grateful for today. This is quite uncommon among other animals on this planet. Human emotions like love or affection are also shared by other living creatures, but the concept of forgiveness is unique to us. That's what sets it apart and makes it almost a divine power.

The process of forgiving or asking for forgiveness is purifying. It's an extremely powerful tool; we can end age-old conflicts with the language of forgiveness. It is also an amazing tool that can make letting go of one's ego as easy as plucking a flower. We live fleeting lives and make many mistakes within them. Why, then, must we hesitate to ask for forgiveness for these mistakes? If you have committed a mistake, admitting it and taking responsibility for your actions is a powerful gesture that can only make you stronger.

I am sure while reading this, certain faces may come to mind–people you felt like asking for forgiveness from but ignored for whatever reason or others you feel you could forgive but are reluctant to. We have an opportunity today, so let's forgive and ask for forgiveness from those people.

* * *

15.

Home: A Sheltering Reminder

In January 2020, I was in Las Vegas, the entertainment capital of the world. Vegas is a magical mirage in the Nevada desert, full of pubs, clubs, and casinos. I was on my way back to the hotel in a car after a meeting, and we were waiting at a signal when I saw a person passing by, shouting something. He had shabby hair, was shirtless, and dressed only in jeans. I thought he was drunk. When I asked the driver, he said, "He is a homeless man, my friend."

I was shocked because I never expected to see a homeless person in the middle of Las Vegas. It's a city of wealth, where every night, people spend millions of dollars in casinos. Over the next few days, I started noticing many untidily dressed people at night. Somehow, they managed to gather 10–15 dollars to enter a McDonald's or a small shop to have a meal, spending as much time as they could inside to escape the cold outside.

It was then that I started thinking about how privileged I am. In Kerala, reports say that there are more than 5 lakh homeless people. In India, it's millions. People wait for the city to sleep to find pavements, roadsides, staircases, railway platforms, and even railway tracks to sleep on between trains.

Today, I am gratefully reminded of how lucky I am to have a home, and I am sure that as you read this, there's a roof over your head and you have a home. Let's embrace our homes!

* * *

16.

Silent Blossoms: Unsung Heroes Of Cleanliness

Today, I reflect on our washroom workers, known worldwide as janitors and in India as housekeeping staff. I have noticed that all washroom workers, regardless of the country, often have the same expressionless face and the same emotion–the same indifference or hesitation.

It seems that no one aspires to be a washroom worker; it's not a job many would consciously choose. These individuals likely ended up in this role due to the circumstances life presented to them. Consider what they do: they clean up the unpleasant waste that we often don't even want to look at. They are the ones who clean our waste in hotels, restaurants, apartments, airports, and other public places.

I'd like to mention something I always try to do and encourage others to do as well. When using a washroom in a hotel or in any other situation, it's a good habit to clean up after ourselves. With just a minute's effort, we can tidy up a bit if we pay attention to it. It's true that these workers are responsible for cleaning the washrooms, no matter how we leave them, but aren't they humans, too? Can't we see them as one of us? We can express a bit of humanity through our actions, can't we?

Today, I remember with gratitude the janitors and housekeepers, the people who cleanse the world of its waste—the silent blossoms.

* * *

17.

Unbreakable Spirit: Lessons From Louis Zamperini

Yesterday, I watched a movie called "Unbroken," which tells the true story of an American Air Force officer named Louis Zamperini during World War II. He was part of a bomber squad whose aircraft crashed in the Pacific Ocean. He survived on a raft with no food, managing to catch some fish and birds and even fighting off a shark. He faced storms and spent almost 47 days on the raft before being captured by the Japanese military. He was then imprisoned in the Marshall Islands in the Pacific. Surprisingly, he was also an Olympian who participated in the 1936 Berlin Olympics, and his extraordinary spirit helped him endure brutal treatment at the hands of the Japanese. After the war, when America defeated Japan, the American army reached Japanese territory and rescued him.

Zamperini's survival in the Pacific Ocean and the brutality he faced while being held captive by the Japanese army are incredibly inspirational in terms of the human ability to endure and perform under the harshest conditions. For thousands of years, our ancestors battled wild animals, the weather, nature, the ice-cold winters, deserts, and oceans. They fought well and kept our species alive. A phenomenal survival instinct is embedded in our genes.

That spirit of survival in human beings, embedded in you and me, to resist, overcome challenges, and transcend resilience is the ability I am grateful for today.

* * *

18.

Candles That Illuminate The Lives Of Others

A couple of years ago, I was traveling by Uber in Bangalore. Just before reaching my destination, I said to my driver, "Bro, you speak really good English."

He had a great command of English, and I appreciated him for it. He responded, "Yes, sir, I happened to study at one of the top schools in the city."

He went on to share that his father had passed away in an accident while he was in the 10th grade. With no relatives to rely on and his mother breaking down and falling ill, he had to drop out of school to start working in order to take care of his mother and support his brother and two sisters. He told me that he had been able to provide his siblings with a good education and had arranged good marriages for his sisters. They were all well-settled now, and his brother was one of the directors of a leading software company in the UK.

As my car approached the destination, I asked the driver, "Brother, out of curiosity, I would like to know how your brother and sisters are with you now. I understand that you probably have different standards of living and are in different social classes, so to speak."

He replied, "They are very kind and loving to me, sir, and we have a harmonious relationship."

I got out of the car and was handing him cash through the window when I noticed, in the light of the traffic, that he had tears in his eyes. Today, let us remember our loved ones who have sacrificed many things in their lives to make ours better. Like candles, they burn themselves to give us light. Let's remember them gratefully and thankfully.

* * *

19.

Echoes Of Yesterday: Embracing The Sum Of Our Past

We don't forget some things. When I was in college, I had a notebook for data structures, and there was a quote on the cover that said, "Today is the sum of all yesterdays." I personally loved that quote, and even after that semester, I would write it in all of my notebooks. Later, I often repeated this quote in various places while engaging with different people. The whole idea was to acknowledge the undeniable reality that we are living in this moment: we can breathe, see things, experience our cognitive functions, perceive the world through our senses, have perspective, possess a body, are alive, and have a mind, intellect, and discernment.

We are the sum of all the yesterdays in our lives; we did not just come into existence this morning. We are a collection, an accumulation, of the years we have been on this planet and our past moments and days! Whatever colors or tones they might be, our yesterdays make us who we are today–we might have won, lost, been happy, experienced sorrows, cheerfully celebrated with friends, lived in solitude, enjoyed the spring, and sweated through the hot summer.

Our yesterdays make us strong and bring meaning to our lives; they collectively create our today, this moment, and this reality. I am repeating the quote again: "Today is the sum of all yesterdays."

I am thankfully remembering all my yesterdays and the fallen leaves with gratitude and love.

* * *

20.

The Legacy Of Sir Nicholas Winton

I recently watched a video from 1988 by the BBC featuring Mr. Nicholas Winton, a famous British banker. During World War II, Mr. Winton rescued some Jewish children from the Nazi Holocaust and helped them find new families in Britain. This heroic act remained unknown to the world for 50 years until his wife, Ms. Grete, found a personal notebook containing the names and photographs of the children he saved. Ms. Grete passed that book to the BBC program, which invited Mr. Winton to appear.

However, Mr. Winton had no idea why the BBC had invited him. During the program, the host said, "We have a list of children rescued by Mr. Winton," and then called out the name "Ms. Vera Gissing," who was present at the program and sitting next to Mr.

Winton–a girl he had rescued 50 years earlier. He was surprised, and Ms. Vera hugged Mr. Winton, creating a very emotional moment as the child met her rescuer after five decades.

The host then addressed the audience, asking, "Is there anyone in our audience tonight who owes their lives to Mr. Nicholas Winton? If so, could you please stand up?" There was a brief silence, during which people looked around at each other. Then, breaking the silence, the whole crowd stood up around Mr. Winton and began clapping their hands.

In total, he had saved 669 human lives from Nazi concentration camps during World War II. He appeared calm and content at that moment. For his great service to humanity, he was knighted "Sir" by Queen Elizabeth II in 2003.

People like Sir Nicholas Winton make us realize how small our contributions to the world may seem and how much more we could do to make it a better place. My gratitude to Sir Nicholas Winton for inspiring me to the core.

* * *

21.

Travel That Unlocks Change

I'm sure more than 90% of the people reading this want or need a change in their lives. It's a fundamental fact that the life we experience is a result of our routines and habits, as discussed in earlier posts like "Break Pattern" and "Habit Loop."

To bring about change, we need to disrupt the system, and one of the best tools for disruption in this context is travel. If we continue living in the same place with the same people, change is unlikely to happen. That's where travel comes in.

Travel to different places, meet new people, explore different perspectives, and experience new things. This wider exposure can help us "crack the nut" and bring about the change we desire.

I still remember a professor in my college who strongly encouraged me to travel for a couple of weeks. He felt I needed a break from my usual patterns to bring about a change in my path. Professors like him are quite rare, I'm sure. His advice had a significant impact on my life, and I'm still a fan of this wonderful tool.

I am grateful for all the travels I have undertaken and the ones yet to come.

** * **

22.

Diversify Your Investments: Eggs And Baskets

I felt I should share some advice I received from one of my mentors. It's not extraordinary or unknown, nor is it overly complicated, but it's something that makes more sense to me as I get older. The advice was: "Do not put all your eggs in one basket." Whether in investments, your career, personal life, entrepreneurship, or even spiritual endeavors, it's important to invest your time and resources sensibly and wisely. Never depend entirely on one option. Let's create a diverse and well-balanced portfolio.

I am grateful to the mentor who constantly reminds me of this wisdom, and I truly hope that all of you give this perspective the attention it deserves to make your lives better.

* * *

23.

Surrender: Guiding You Through Unknown Chapters

In the journey of life, we often encounter chapters we have yet to live or pass by. These moments can be both surprising and confusing, especially when we must make choices in the unknown, unread chapters of our lives. One of the finest torches we can carry on such dark, unclear paths is our ability to surrender ourselves to something beyond us.

Surrender is not giving up; it is an absolute submission of ourselves to someone or something we trust. It may be the universe, nature, your gut feelings, karma, or your mentors. It could be anything in which you have great confidence, to which you surrender yourself completely and walk the path. Surprisingly, even when you are unaware of the context, your choices often turn out right and improve your life. My gratitude goes to the mentor who shared this insight and helped me understand the power of surrendering!

* * *

24.

Inspiration Everywhere: Finding Motivation In The World Around Us

The other day, I was having a conversation with a group of college students about entrepreneurship. It was more of a Q&A session, and a student asked me, "How do you find your inspiration? How do you keep yourself motivated?"

It was actually the first time I had thought about it! I paused for a moment and then told her, "I don't know if it's a condition, but I have this tendency to find an element of inspiration in almost everything around me. The whole world inspires me."

Today, I happened to read about a Brazilian couple who planted 2.7 million trees over 20 years! I was incredibly thrilled and genuinely inspired. At that moment, I recalled that student's question.

Today, I extend my gratitude to the Brazilian couple, Sebastião Salgado and his wife, Lélia Deluiz Wanick Salgado, for inspiring me to build things larger than life!

* * *

25.

Rich Dad Poor Dad

Today, I received a memory notification from Facebook from seven years ago! It was a post in which I mentioned that I was reading the book *Rich Dad, Poor Dad* and quoted the following sentence: "People's lives are forever controlled by two emotions: fear and greed. Those who overcome them will master money."

As I grow older, this perspective makes even more sense to me. *Rich Dad, Poor Dad* is one of my all-time favorite books. When I had zero education about finance, this book was a treasure for me. It helped me understand the fundamental differences between an asset and a liability.

Today, I'm gratefully remembering Robert Kiyosaki, the author of this insightful book.

* * *

26.

True Richness: Beyond The Illusion Of Wealth

In life, the choice between being truly rich and merely appearing rich is an age-old paradox.

The richness I'm referring to goes beyond financial or economic well-being. It includes our emotional well-being, social values, education, satisfaction in our profession, and even the number of genuine friends we have. We can either be genuinely rich or merely act as if we are.

Pretending to be rich or bluffing to impress others results in a miserable life. If we ever find ourselves pretending to be rich in any aspect of our lives, it's time to stop and start pursuing true richness.

While the concept is simple, implementing it can be challenging due to societal norms of wealth.

I am grateful for this very genuine idea.

* * *

27.

The Temple Of The Heart

The other day, I was watching a much-anticipated Indian anthology series (in Tamil) on Netflix. The variety of talents coming together and the very purpose of creating such a project amidst the pandemic was exciting. The producers created this project to support daily-wage workers and other members of the Film Employees Federation of South India affected by the COVID-19 pandemic.

The first episode of the anthology highlighted the significance of empathy, which we must carry in our hearts as humans. One perspective shared in that episode truly touched me. It said, "A man could become God when his heart becomes a temple."

It was simple, serene, and profoundly right.

My gratitude to the makers of that episode.

* * *

28.

The Mystery Of 'Empty Eye'

During the final year of my engineering course, I did my main project in Hyderabad. With plenty of free time, I decided to look for a part-time job. After several searches, I found a technology company that aligned with my interest in network security. The company developed and sold network security products to the US and UK markets. I passed the technical interview with ease and then had another interview to assess my general proficiency. I was damn confident during and after the interview, but later, they informed me that I was not selected. When I asked for the reason, they said I had an 'Empty Eye' while speaking English. I told the lady that, fortunately, I had no problem with my eyes, and she repeated, "You have got an empty eye." I insisted that I could see things and there was no problem, but she yelled, "Empty eye, empty eye, empty eye!" and hung up the phone!

I had no idea what 'Empty Eye' meant, and after asking many friends–including a medical student–who were all clueless, I remained puzzled. A few years later, a friend who is an entrepreneur invited me to join a hiring session at his company for a day. I participated in it, and we were four members involved in a techno-commercial role. During the candidate shortlisting after the interviews, when I suggested a profile, my friend said, "He's a good candidate, but he has an empty eye, which might be a problem in international sales."

My memory of the rejection came rushing back, and I asked him, "Bro, what the *%*$ is this 'Empty Eye'?"

After a pause, he calmly explained, "Bro, it's Mother Tongue Influence–MTI!" I was left speechless for a few minutes!

Today, when I met that friend again, I recalled this memory. My gratitude to him for clarifying my years-old doubt about 'Empty Eye'!

* * *

29.

No Half Measures, Period

When we implement a new system, policy, or resource in an organization–or even in our personal lives–the success of that implementation depends on how effectively we leverage it toward the larger goal. If we find that the system, policy, or resource is not delivering the desired results, it often indicates that we were not strict enough in its implementation.

Reading a blog on Strategy made me consider this perspective. If you want to bring about disruptive changes, there are no half measures.

My gratitude to the blogger who shared this perspective.

* * *

30.

An Unforgettable Meal From An Angel In The Skies

Just before the lockdown, I was flying from Mumbai to Bangalore and noticed the cabin crew serving meals to passengers. Since the meal was included in my ticket, I waited for my turn. I overheard the cabin crew mention that the options were vegetable pulao with roti or chicken curry. I decided to choose roti and chicken curry.

When the cabin crew reached me, she served the pulao. I asked her, "I heard you have chicken curry and roti. Could I have that instead?"

She replied, "Sir, our non-vegetarian option is finished; only the vegetarian pulao is available."

I requested, "Could you check with your colleague?" since another crew member had a different pantry wagon. She checked and confirmed that no non-vegetarian meals were available.

I said, "Okay, fine. I'm not that hungry; I'll just have some water." I really didn't feel like having the vegetable pulao.

After serving the rest of the passengers, the crew member returned to me in about 15 minutes and handed me the meal I had originally wanted. I was surprised.

As I was disembarking in Bangalore, I saw the crew member waiting near the exit. Out of curiosity, I asked her, "You told me there were no non-vegetarian meals available. How did you get one for me?"

She replied, "Sir, I hope you enjoyed the meal."

I told her I did. She smiled and said, "Sir, actually, the cabin crew has a meal allocation, and I had opted for the non-veg option, so it was my meal that I gave to you."

Although it was a small gesture, this incident touched me deeply. Today, as I am back in Mumbai and reflecting on my previous flight experience, I am gratefully remembering the cabin crew member who gave her meal to me.

Note:

This story was originally posted on my blog on the 27th of January 2021. We later noticed a similar scene in the Hindi movie Chor Nikal Ke Bhaga, which was released in March 2023. While I believe this may be a mere coincidence, I wanted to inform my readers that the blog was published first.

* * *

31.

Be Intentionally Deaf When You Move Forward

A friend of mine was hosting a clubhouse session on Undivided Attention. I couldn't join it, so I later asked him to share the essence of the session with me. He told me just one thing: "Be intentionally deaf while driving towards your goal." I found this advice both sensible and enlightening.

When we have the control to choose whose voice enters our mind (by being intentionally deaf), our energy won't be wasted on counterarguments or other distractions while heading towards our destination. It's a simple thought expressed beautifully.

My gratitude goes to the friend who shared this idea with me.

* * *

32.

Simply Vanilla

In the English language, the word "Vanilla" is often used to describe something ordinary or lacking distinction. Its meanings include being very plain, conventional, or common. However, I don't underestimate the taste of vanilla, which is my favorite flavor. Whether in ice cream, drinks, cakes, or any edible item, I always prefer vanilla for its calm, content, and balanced nature rather than extreme tastes. Vanilla always brings a sense of balance and satisfaction.

Vanilla has never disappointed me, and I've never lost interest in it despite consuming it more than any other flavor in my life. Today, I extend my gratitude to Vanilla for all the delightful experiences it has provided me.

* * *

33.
Fashion Model

Over three years ago, I had an executive assistant who performed exceptionally well in the interview, which led me to hire him. He mentioned his interest in business development and strategy, particularly in the media and entertainment industry.

An EA must be very flexible, especially when he's supporting a startup entrepreneur. Although he was doing well and trying his best to adapt to my working style, I sensed that he was not entirely satisfied with his job.

I asked him about it multiple times, but he insisted he was content. His probation period was three months, but I decided to ask him to leave before he completed even a month. I felt he was searching for something else and encouraged him to reflect and pursue what he truly wanted.

Three years later, I noticed his Instagram account and was thrilled to see that he had found his path! His account was filled with dances, martial arts, workouts, and photoshoots. Most interestingly, his profile stated "Fashion Model."

Looking back, I feel grateful for the decision I made that day to ask him to leave and find his true path. Although he seemed sad at the time, his current pictures radiate cheerfulness and joy!

* * *

34.

A Spoonful Of Kindness: A Sweet Childhood Memory

This happened in 1999 when I was nine years old. It was my first school outing–a day trip from Kozhikode to Wayanad and back. In the evening, as we were about to board the bus home, we noticed an ice cream stall. Someone asked the teacher, a nun, "Sister, can we go and buy ice cream?"

She hesitated but said, "Okay, we're almost done. You can buy ice cream, but make it quick."

The note given to parents strictly stated that no outside purchases were allowed. I didn't have a single penny in my pocket, and I assumed that no one else did either. However, I saw everyone pulling out money and heading to the ice cream stall. Feeling sad and shy, I thought, "I have no money, but I love ice cream!"

I stayed behind, sitting on a bench under a tree, while my friends rushed to the stall. The nun came over and asked, "Amarnath, why don't you buy yourself ice cream? It's okay."

I smiled, but I couldn't bring myself to tell her I had no money. It probably never even crossed her mind. Then, one of my classmates looked at me from the stall and came over, asking, "Shall I buy ice cream for you?"

I replied, "No, it's okay."

When he asked why, I lied and said I had tonsillitis, so I couldn't have ice cream. He insisted that nothing would happen if I had ice cream just for one day. He took a spoonful of ice cream from his cup and told me to eat a little, saying, "Nothing will happen; just have it for me." I took a spoonful and thanked him as he smiled and walked away.

Looking back, I had never experienced such empathy from someone my own age until that day. I gratefully remember that friend, the 9-year-old boy. It was the cherry on top of the picnic.

* * *

35.

A Gamble Wheel On The Question Paper

This happened while I was studying at an entrance coaching center in Thrissur, Kerala, during my 12th standard. I thought that if I paid less attention to my 12th-grade schoolwork and focused on entrance exam preparation, I could get through. But after a couple of weeks of classes, I realized that it wouldn't be easy to crack the examination unless I performed well in the 12th. Eventually, I lost interest in the entrance exam and began watching movies and exploring Thrissur.

My roommate, who was also my friend, always accompanied me but somehow managed to get decent marks. So, I asked him, "Bro, you're with me all the time, but how do you manage to do well?"

He said, "Bro, I'm doing the 'Karakikuth.'" (Karakikuth literally means throwing darts at a spinning wheel, akin to taking a gamble.)

I told him, "Okay, I'll do that too."

To my surprise, my scores started to fall. I used to score around 50 or 60 out of 100, but after starting the Karakikuth, I began getting 20 or 30, while my friend scored 70 or 80. I didn't understand what was happening since we were both following the same approach. After two weeks, he noticed one of my test papers and saw that I had drawn a wheel on the question paper, divided it into five options from A to E, and marked the wheel with many dots.

He asked me what that was, and I explained that I had drawn a wheel on the question paper for the Karakikuth. He asked, "Is this what you understood by Karakikuth? What I meant by Karakikuth was 'guesswork.' Look at the options, apply common sense, and make an educated guess. You'll be able to pick the relatively right answers."

He came from a different part of Kerala where "Karakikuth" meant "guesswork," a meaning I wasn't familiar with. I had been literally trying to replicate throwing darts at a wheel on my answer sheet with a pen, which led to my repeated failures for a couple of weeks.

There are experiences in our lives where we find ourselves doing foolish things, but when we look back, they make us laugh out loud. Today, let's be thankful for those experiences that make us laugh at our own stupidity.

* * *

36.

Being In The Flow Of Life

We have two ways to live life. One is by crafting it like an architect–manifesting, scheduling, setting goals, and overcoming obstacles to build the life we want. However, I don't believe it's possible for people to craft 100% of their lives. It is possible to the extent that human beings have that much potential, which is incredible.

The other way of living is by letting things happen. If we consider everything to be a system–we and the people around us are systems, society is a system, the Earth is a system contained within the solar system, and the whole universe is a system–we live in systems within systems. Whether we consciously craft life or not, we exist within a flow that is a result of the influence of all these systems.

The second option of letting things happen, existing within the flow, is like being in a boat with an oar, making sure that the boat sails smoothly over twists and turns without much involvement or aggressiveness. Just being, witnessing, and letting things happen in the flow is more poetic and mystical.

In Sanskrit, there is a phrase "Anuugacchati Pravaha," which means being within the cosmic flow of life. Many people in the world, consciously or not, choose this way of living, which is also beautiful. It's up to you whether you want to be an architect, a poet, or a mystic; that's your choice.

Today, I am grateful for this beautiful, poetic, and mystical idea of being in the flow.

* * *

37.

Curiosity And The Rewarding Circuit In The Brain

We often hear that one of the best ways to lead a fulfilling life is by maintaining our childlike qualities. In my view, while this perspective might be broad, the most intriguing quality to retain as a powerful tool is curiosity.

When you observe a child, their eyes are always wide open, and the world around them is full of wonder—every sound, smell, taste, and sight is perceived as new and fascinating. Children ask numerous questions: Why is the sky blue? Why does the moon seem to follow us? Why do fruits always fall down? Why does the sun disappear at night? As adults, however, we often lose this sense of curiosity.

Humans have a lifetime to gather information and understand both ourselves and the world. Yet, as we start to ignore the unknown, our curiosity gradually diminishes.

I recently read in a journal that, psychologically, curiosity is closely linked to the rewarding circuit in our brains. When we encounter something unclear and seek information to understand it, our brains release dopamine, which makes us feel fantastic.

In essence, let's approach the world without prejudice or ignorance. Let's ask questions, learn more about our surroundings, enjoy the dopamine rewards, and feel fantastic.

Today, I express my gratitude for the remarkable quality of the human brain–the urge to know, which is curiosity.

* * *

38.

Understanding Loss Aversion

I listened to a professor deliver a lecture on management studies, where he explained a very interesting concept: Loss Aversion.

This concept is directly related to behavioral finance and suggests that the psychological pain of losing is about twice as powerful as the pleasure of gaining. For example, the pain of losing $100 is roughly twice as intense as the pleasure of gaining $100.

Daniel Kahneman, who researched this concept, received the Nobel Memorial Prize in 2002. It's a perspective widely used in marketing techniques for products and services around the world. Offers, rebates, and pricing strategies used by companies are often based on this psychological reality.

I find this perspective to be truly fascinating. Understanding this as a consumer can help us manage our behavior better when making purchases.

Today, I extend my gratitude to the professor who shared this valuable insight with me.

* * *

39.
Sailing

I still remember a day in school when I had a headache from the paint fumes lingering in my house after it had been painted the previous day. It was before lunch break, and the teacher asked us about our ambitions and what we wanted to become in life. My friends had different choices: some wanted to join the Indian Army, others aspired to be doctors, engineers, businessmen, or advocates. One guy even said he wanted to become a JCB driver. A friend of mine stood up and said he'd like to be a painter. I didn't like his choice.

I knew that his father was a mason, so during the lunch break, I approached him and said, "Bro, I know your father is struggling as a construction laborer, supporting you and your family, but I didn't like your choice of profession today. You're studying at a great institution; you should think bigger. There are vast possibilities for professions. You need to move beyond your current mindset and think of something more than becoming a painter."

He paused for a moment and replied, "Dude, I didn't mean that kind of painting job. Do you know Da Vinci and Michelangelo? I want to become a painter like them; that's what I meant." He laughed at me and walked away.

I felt ashamed that day for judging my friend. Knowing his family background, I had subconsciously convinced myself that he could only aspire to paint houses. In reality, he was thinking much beyond that. Life is full of possibilities, and every person has the potential to dream and achieve whatever they choose. That experience taught me a lifetime lesson: Being non-judgmental opens up greater possibilities. Today, I am gratefully remembering the value of being non-judgmental.

P.S. My friend didn't become a house painter or an artist, but a sailor. Today, he's celebrating on a cruise ship anchored somewhere in the Caribbean Islands.

* * *

40.

Rasam: The Magical Recipe

Today was quite a busy day, and it was only by 3:30 PM that I found a restaurant for lunch. It was a Tamil vegetarian restaurant. I asked for a meal, but they said they were out of those and advised me to try the tiffin instead. I knew the guy and asked him what it included. He said it came with white rice, rasam, pappadam, pickles, curd, and bean thoran. I agreed, and he served me a wonderful lunch.

I have always been amazed by the magic of rasam–it's a delightful soup dish. With a good rasam, you can have a satisfying meal with just a pappadam, thoran, and pickle. Rasam also has great medicinal properties, as it's made with tamarind, turmeric, tomato, chili pepper, cumin, garlic, black pepper, black mustard, curry leaves, coriander leaves, and various other ingredients.

It's a home remedy for common colds, especially among South Indians.

When we were children, our elders would make rasam to cure common colds and fevers. Rasam has many magical properties–it helps reduce blood sugar levels, making it suitable for diabetic patients, serves as a treatment for anemia, it is a powerful antioxidant, helps the body combat free radicals, and prevents constipation. It's a comprehensive remedy, particularly valuable for building immunity in the midst of the COVID-19 pandemic.

I don't know who was that magician who created this magical formula with such great taste and remarkable medicinal effects. Let's try to include rasam in our diet, especially during these times.

Today, I am lovingly and gratefully remembering this wonderful dish–Rasam.

* * *

41.

Unlove: A Liberation From Limiting Love

Love is one of the most beautiful feelings in life, but even when it is genuine, it can sometimes limit us. Whether it's love for a person, a place, a profession, an ideology, or a habit, when a feeling begins to overrule your genuine interests, it indicates that something needs to be addressed.

I have always wondered why people haven't figured out a perfect antidote for love when it becomes toxic. While hate is often considered the opposite of love, I am personally not a fan of it. Hatred is a negative, self-destructive emotion. That's where "unlove" comes in.

If a person, thing, place, or habit you love limits your possibilities, then unloving is what you need to do–it's like unplugging but without hating.

I truly believe that the art of unloving could resolve many problems in our lives.

Today, I am grateful for this incredible idea!

* * *

42.

Matrix Defines Purpose

Like many of you, the Matrix trilogy is one of my all-time favorite movie series. Over the past two decades, I have watched the trilogy many times, and each time I find new meanings and dimensions in it. The movies depict an imaginary future where machines dominate and enslave humanity. They also explore numerous layers of meaning, from the metaphysical to the spiritual.

One of the finest lines from the movie that always resonates with me is: "It is the purpose that created us, purpose that connects us, purpose that pulls us, that guides us, that drives us; it is purpose that defines us, purpose that binds us."

These lines encapsulate the essence of our existence on this planet. With deep love and respect, I am gratefully remembering Lana and Lilly Wachowski for this profound narrative and the ultimate cinematic experience they have provided us.

* * *

43.

Attitude Of Being A Custodian

One of the most compelling perspectives in Eastern philosophy is the idea of being a custodian. I believe that the awareness of being a custodian can resolve almost every problem and challenge encountered in life. Whatever we acquire or have with us is ours for only a specific span of time. Before us, it belonged to someone else, and after us, it will go to another.

Wars, conflicts, rat races, unhealthy competition, crime, guilt, greed, and envy—all these negative emotions arise when we ignorantly believe that we or someone else possess something forever. In reality, nobody does. Such feelings can ultimately cause us harm or bury us. We carry nothing permanently; we haven't carried anything permanently, and we won't carry anything permanently. Today, I felt compelled to express my gratitude for this insightful perspective on Eastern philosophy.

* * *

44.

When Emojis Disrupted The Way We Communicate

Studies show that body language constitutes almost 55 percent of communication. From facial expressions to the direction in which our feet are positioned during a conversation, everything framed by our body is considered nonverbal communication.

In the digital era, nonverbal communication has found a significant counterpart in emoticons, emojis, or smileys. The history of smileys began in the early '80s and gained popularity with the evolution of GUIs (graphical user interfaces). They have become ubiquitous in the internet and post-internet eras.

Scientists have found that when a person receives an emoji, the emotion generated in the brain is akin to seeing the actual facial expression of the individual.

Even though it's not real, the emotional impact is almost the same, providing a meaningful emotional experience through digital nonverbal communication. It is also noted that more expressive people tend to use more emojis in their conversations.

Emojis have become an integral part of our daily lives. I think it's worth expressing our gratitude for these small, beautiful icons that add a new dimension to our communication in today's world.

* * *

45.

Guru Dispels The Darkness Of Ignorance

When we look at great leaders like Alexander, Chandragupta, Isaac Newton, Leonardo da Vinci, Jawaharlal Nehru, Pele, Sachin Tendulkar, Steve Jobs, and others, we find that they all had great mentors who played a crucial role in shaping their success.

A mentor (or guru, in Indian terms) is akin to a kingmaker who can foresee things and guide their disciples in the right direction, helping them achieve their goals. In Asian cultures, especially in India, there is immense respect for gurus, mentors, and masters. Even in royal courts, the Raj Guru (the king's mentor) was considered above the king. Today is Guru Purnima, a day celebrated widely across the Indian subcontinent and among various religions and communities, honoring one's mentors and masters who dispel the darkness of ignorance.

I am grateful to the Guru Parampara (the lineage of masters and mentors) who have helped me emerge from the darkness of ignorance over time.

* * *

46.

We Can Wait A Minute

This evening, while driving back from Lulu Mall, I encountered a traffic jam at a junction. The noise of horns and shouting suggested a serious issue, but it turned out to be something different.

A woman, around 50 years old, was struggling to make a U-turn. It was clear from her gestures that she was inexperienced and new to driving. She repeatedly tried to start the car but couldn't manage the clutch properly, causing the car to stall. The frustration of the drivers around her was palpable. An autorickshaw driver eventually stepped in, drove her car across the road, and parked it. The crowd dispersed, and the woman walked away, visibly distressed.

This incident made me reflect on the behavior of drivers. Those of us who drive regularly can often tell if someone is inexperienced. Once we recognize this, there seems little point in honking, shouting, and making the person feel ashamed and fearful.

I imagine she felt very bad, nervous, and disappointed, and she might even be discouraged from driving in the future. Can't we show a bit more compassion? She was trying to learn something new. Why not appreciate her effort and wait a minute in solidarity rather than ridicule her?

We all learn skills in this manner, often facing challenges and relying on the patience of others. Today, let's remember with gratitude those who have helped us excel and those who patiently waited for us to develop our skills.

* * *

47.

Legend Of Field Marshal Sam Manekshaw

Field Marshal Sam Manekshaw is one of the most distinguished names in Indian military history. His legacy spans from World War II to the 1971 Indo-Pakistani War during the Bangladesh Liberation War, where India achieved a decisive victory against Pakistan, capturing 93,000 soldiers, liberating Bangladesh, and subsequently releasing all those captured soldiers back to Pakistan. The country honored him with the Padma Vibhushan, and he was the first army officer to receive the title of Field Marshal.

There is a story about his time in a hospital in Coonoor, near Ooty. At that time, Dr. A.P.J. Abdul Kalam was the President of India and visited Coonoor. Upon learning that Manekshaw was in the military hospital there, Dr. Kalam decided to meet the legend. The visit was unscheduled, so things were hurried, but Dr. Kalam was determined to meet Manekshaw.

Dr. Kalam spent some time with the hero, who was bedridden, and they discussed many topics. Just before leaving, Dr. Kalam asked Manekshaw, "Are you comfortable here? Is there anything I can do to make your situation better? Do you have any grievances or needs that could make you more comfortable?"

After a long pause, Manekshaw replied, "Your Excellency, I have one grievance."

Dr. Kalam was shocked and asked, "What is it?"

Manekshaw said, "Sir, my grievance is that I am unable to get up from this bed and salute the respected President of my beloved country. That is the only grievance I have."

Dr. Kalam held Manekshaw's hand, and both were moved to tears. This story exemplifies how Manekshaw remained dedicated to his duty even in his final days. Legends like Manekshaw have shaped our country into what it is today. Today, with gratitude, let's remember Field Marshal Sam Manekshaw.

* * *

48.

Goddess Of Grace: A Teacher's Gift On Onam

Onam is the most widely celebrated festival in the Indian state of Kerala. People create flower carpets at homes, offices, and institutions to welcome prosperity and the mythical King Mahabali. On the day of the Onam celebration at school, students were required to bring flowers to class to make the flower carpet. We enjoyed the process, and there was also a competition to see which class made the best flower carpet.

I was in the 2nd grade at the time. The day before the celebration, I collected some beautiful flowers from our backyard and the paddy field, eagerly preparing for the event. However, on the day of the celebration, I forgot to bring the flowers to school.

When I arrived at school, I realized the flowers were missing from my bag. My friends were excitedly showing off the flowers they had brought, while I felt sad and disappointed. As the students began drawing designs and arranging their flowers for the carpet, I sat away, feeling dejected. My teacher noticed and asked why I was sitting idle and where my flowers were. With guilt, I explained that I had forgotten them at home.

She smiled warmly, took me to the staff room, and gave me a bunch of beautiful violet flowers of Asian pigeonwings, asking me to join my friends in making the flower carpet. To me, she felt like a goddess, and I felt truly blessed! I joined my friends with a great sense of honor.

Looking back, it was a small incident, but the 8-year-old boy in me cherished it for a lifetime. My gratitude to the teacher for her wonderful gesture that day! It's amazing how little acts of kindness leave a lasting impact on children. Have a happy Onam, everyone!

* * *

49.

Niyyah: The Purpose Behind Every Action

Yesterday, I had a discussion with a friend about the different systems we build in life, whether they be organizations or engagements with people. All of these systems rely on a set of actions. A point my friend brought up was an Arabic word called "Niyyah."

Niyyah, or Niyat, refers to the ultimate purpose behind every establishment. Whenever we build a system–whatever it may be–the actions we carry out within it should have a clear purpose. The future of that particular action or system depends entirely on the Niyyah behind it. This purpose cannot be understood by others because it is defined by us.

The actions we take must have a purpose, and that purpose is determined solely by us. The result or future of the action or system depends on how clear and steadfast the Niyyah is.

He also advised that once we establish a system with a Niyyah, we should not alter it as time goes by, as such changes could compromise the outcome of the system.

This concept, though familiar to me, was presented in a new light through a new term in a different language. It was quite eye-opening in the context of our discussion.

I am truly grateful to my friend for introducing me to the concept of Niyyah and enlightening me while I was in a state of confusion.

* * *

50.

Musa The Trillionaire: Emperor Of The Salt

As an entrepreneur whose enterprise falls under the services category, I have always admired entrepreneurs who deal with consumer goods–specifically B2C products–because the potential in that area of business is immense. I recently read an article from the BBC about the richest man in modern history–West African ruler Mansa Musa, who lived in the 14th century. His empire was called the Mali Empire, and during his time, he possessed a trillion-dollar fortune when adjusted to today's currency values.

His predominant business was selling salt and gold. He controlled about 50% of the entire salt trade in the world at that time. It's fascinating to think about how salt–a simple, basic element used in every household–was so central to his empire in the 14th century. This serves as a true inspiration for entrepreneurs who create products that can be sold to billions of people worldwide. Today, I extend my gratitude to all those visionaries who built empires by creating and selling consumer goods across the globe.

* * *

51.

The Power Of Undivided Attention

Andrew Carnegie, an American business magnate, was one of the richest people in history. His life story is captivating and a classic example of the American Dream. He was the son of a migrant, worked in various industries, and later built one of the most successful business empires of all time.

People, as well as the government, were suspicious of Carnegie's success due to his exponential growth. The US Senate even interrogated him about how he managed and ran his business. He said, "I can keep my mind focused on something for five minutes at a stretch." The members thought it sounded simple, so Carnegie set up an experiment, but they couldn't even maintain their attention for a few seconds.

It was, in fact, his ability to give undivided attention to tasks that contributed to his exponential growth. I read a blog today that shared this interesting story about Andrew Carnegie, who has always been one of my favorite entrepreneurs. Today, I'm extending my gratitude to the author of the blog who introduced me to this story.

* * *

52.

Parallel Tracks Of Influence: Balancing Forces In History

If you pay close attention to history, you can see that in all times there have been legends and thought leaders who massively influenced people. At the same time, there were also parallel ideologies and perceptions that ran counter to the main, celebrated leader.

Although these parallel figures attracted followers, their controversial or unapproved points led to the rise of alternative leaders. I personally believe that such parallel tracks are necessary to balance the systems in which we live, whether in government, social structures, ideologies, political pathways, or other areas.

A classic example of parallel tracks in the Indian freedom movement is Mahatma Gandhi, a giant figure of his time, and, alongside him, Netaji Subhash

Chandra Bose. Both aimed to achieve the same result—an independent India. While both sought to free India from British rule, they pursued different methods.

The details of their approaches are well known, but the existence of a parallel track like Subhash Chandra Bose's provided significant equilibrium to the history of modern India. Our personal choices, desires, dreams, and the destinations we strive for are also, knowingly or unknowingly, influenced by these parallel tracks that we encounter.

Today, I am gratefully remembering all the parallel tracks and those who were brave enough to stand tall, hold their heads high, and question in pursuit of greater clarity toward common goals.

* * *

53.

Tamil: Language Of The Heart

Last night, while I was at the departure terminal of Dubai airport, I had an argument with my airline operators because they rescheduled my flight from another emirate, Sharjah, to the next day!

During the quarrel, I noticed a woman, about 35 years old, who appeared frightened, shivering, and crying. She was trying to explain things to the officers, but they couldn't understand her, and she became numb.

The officers spoke to her in English, Arabic, Hindi, and broken Malayalam, but she couldn't respond. She appeared beaten up, with fresh scars on her face and was full of fear. She was about to go to Mumbai, and when I looked at her boarding pass, I saw she had a connecting flight from Mumbai to Chennai. I assumed she was a Tamil lady. When I started speaking to her in broken Tamil, she began responding in Tamil.

I learned that she had been trapped in Dubai on a labor visa and had endured physical abuse and domestic violence from her sponsors. In her words, it was like being in prison, and she had somehow managed to get to the airport. She wanted to communicate with her family but had no balance on her phone, no money, and was completely abandoned.

The main problem was that every passenger going to India must carry an Air Suvidha (self-declaration) document, and there was a discrepancy between her actual PNR number and the PNR number mentioned on the Air Suvidha document given by her agent. She had only 35 minutes to board.

In her distress, she said it was better for her to die than to stay back in the UAE. The officers couldn't understand Tamil, so I tried to translate for them. Meanwhile, they were busy with their tasks. I could have created a new Air Suvidha document for her, but my laptop battery was drained.

Despite having a flight from Sharjah in 10 hours, I decided to help her because I knew how to edit the Air Suvidha document. It was a challenging situation, but another officer arranged a laptop for me to work on while she continued to cry and appeared dizzy. I feared she might lose consciousness. Fortunately, I was able to edit and reproduce her Air Suvidha document with the help of the airline staff, and we successfully got her on the flight to her hometown.

I was frustrated when my flight was rescheduled to Sharjah the next day, but I felt content because if my flight hadn't been rescheduled, I wouldn't have been able to help that innocent, tortured, and helpless person.

As she boarded her flight, I asked her name, and she told me it was Mary. She said, "Intha udavi nan markkave maatte" (I will never forget the help that you extended to me).

Having spent almost four years in Tamil Nadu and learning technical engineering there, I realize that, above all my professional qualifications, my command of Tamil helped me execute this divine plan last night. I truly feel that I should extend my gratitude to Tamil Nadu, which has made me a slightly more refined human being through the events of the past day.

* * *

54.

Beyond The Physical: Exploring Receptivity

In science, we learn that there are two properties of nature at the atomic scale: physical (particle) and wave. This concept is quite similar to the human body. According to many metaphysical perspectives, the energy body, or emotional body, has more receptivity than our physical body.

One simple example is that when people close to you, such as friends or relatives, experience an incident that disturbs their internal energy or emotional balance, you might feel the ripples of their emotions even if you are hundreds or thousands of kilometers away. If you later talk to that individual and ask them about what happened, both of you may sense that you experienced a kind of disturbance.

What I understand from this is that the more we make our physical, mental, and energy bodies receptive to such phenomena, the more we will be able to sense things beyond our primary senses.

I have personally experienced many such instances, and today, I felt I should extend my gratitude for my receptivity to perceive and feel things beyond physical distances.

* * *

55.

Inclusive Innovation: Lessons From Hong Kong

In 2015, I visited Hong Kong for the first time. My partner and I were there for discussions with manufacturing facilities and were also associated with one of the largest startup ecosystem enablers in Hong Kong. When I visited the facility, the first thing that struck me was how everything was designed to be user-friendly for differently-abled people–from the roads and entrances to the elevators and walls, there were exclusive tracks and accommodations for those with disabilities.

Instructions were written in Braille on the walls. We observed differently-abled entrepreneurs moving around and interacting within the facility with ease. Additionally, one of the highest-performing startups in the ecosystem was led by differently-abled young people. Recently, the government has been seeking input from entrepreneurs to create new policies for the startup ecosystem. I was fortunate enough to provide some suggestions, and this particular observation was a primary talking point in my recommendations for policy-making. My personal suggestion was to focus on constructing infrastructure and facilities that benefit differently-abled individuals.

I believe it's high time we understood and practiced such inclusiveness in society and tapped into the potential of differently-abled people. Today, I am gratefully reflecting on that facility in Hong Kong, which truly inspired me to frame this perspective as a human being.

* * *

56.

Kuyili: The Immortal Warrior of Sivaganga

The land of Madurai in Tamil Nadu is rich in history, tradition, and valor in war. I once lived in a village called Kaliyarkoil, which was part of the former province of Madurai. Many stories from that land have touched me deeply.

One such story is about the 18th-century Adi Dravida warrior, Kuyili, who was the commander of the army of the queen of Sivaganga. She was known and praised for her intelligence and fearlessness on the battlefield.

During a time of continuous conflict between the British and the kingdom of Sivaganga, the queen's army needed to breach the Sivaganga fort, which had been captured by the British. Kuyili knew she could ensure victory for Sivaganga. On the night of Vijayadashami, under the pretext of attending the temple celebration, she infiltrated the fort and discovered that the British ammunition was stored behind the main temple. She applied oil all over her body, set herself on fire, and went to where the ammunition was kept. Her act led to the complete destruction of the ammunition and ensured the queen's victory against the British. This was the first suicide attack in the history of India, carried out by a woman who sacrificed herself in the fight against the British.

The actions and sacrifices of people like Kuyili have had a ripple effect, significantly contributing to the reality, social systems, and democracy we experience today. Many Adi Dravidas and marginalized individuals gave their lives in the fight against foreign invaders and silently contributed to shaping the future of our country. Often, they are forgotten, while other privileged legends receive more recognition.

Today, with respect and gratitude, I remember the immortal Adi Dravida warrior, Kuyili.

* * *

57.

Embracing The Subtle Extraordinary

We experience the world through our senses—our capacity to see, hear, touch, taste, and smell. Each of our sensory organs has a broad spectrum of receptivity. There is a Zen practice in which you pay attention to your environment by concentrating on very minute details with your senses, offering a beautiful experience of life.

For example, when we use the sense of touch–whether holding a phone, using a laptop, writing something, or holding a glass of water–we experience that touch, but we can experience it in a more profound way. When you touch what you're wearing, paying deep attention allows you to feel the texture of the fabric. It's the same when touching the petals of a flower; that kind of intense attention helps us appreciate the extraordinary capacity of our sense of touch.

Similarly, when we eat, we try to smell the food and extract different fragrant elements from it. Chewing slowly and experiencing the explosion of taste on your taste buds while trying to differentiate each flavor creates a new experience. When observing something, such as a leaf, understand the perfection of its design at a micro level and examine its underside. Just like our fingerprints, the back of every leaf is unique. Observing it helps us appreciate the ultimate sophistication of its design.

When it comes to hearing, sit quietly and listen to the sounds of your body. In a silent place, you may hear faint sounds inside your body. Try to listen to the subtle noises around you—perhaps a distant song, the chirping of birds, or other faint sounds. Experience the broad capacity of your sense of hearing. Today, let's give more attention to the micro, the small things through which we experience the world around us, and be grateful for the small particles that enable the manifestation of the larger physical and sensory experiences we have in life.

* * *

58.
Humans Of Tokyo

I was in Tokyo, Japan, at the beginning of this year. I was busy during the day and didn't have much time to relax in the evenings because most hotels, restaurants, and shops close around 8:30–9 p.m. One night, when I wasn't feeling sleepy at around 2 a.m., I decided to go out for a walk.

I googled and found a restaurant famous for its ramen. It was winter and ice-cold, and the restaurant was quite small, accommodating only around 10–15 people around a U-shaped table. I entered and sat down, surrounded by Japanese patrons who were talking, laughing, and celebrating something I didn't understand. I just ordered ramen.

I noticed various dishes on the tables, and one item looked like a starfish–very beautiful. I couldn't resist asking the person sitting to my left what it was. He placed a piece of starfish on my plate and encouraged me to try it. I felt a bit embarrassed, but it was delicious. In his broken English, he asked me, “Where are you from?” I replied, “I am from India.”

He shouted something to his friends, who were a team, and they started speaking and laughing among themselves. Even the cook, who was cooking and serving, laughed and said something. Then, the cook began cleaning up my part of the table and started bringing in plates of different dishes.

Everyone on that team ordered their favorite dishes and asked me to taste them. I must have tried almost every dish in the restaurant by 2:30 a.m. They served me excellent drinks, took photos with me, and even settled my bill. They gave me wonderful memories and great-tasting food, and I have immense respect for the people of Japan.

I'm sharing this story because they gave me such memorable experiences. I don't know their names or who they are, but their kindness and effort to make me feel included and positive about their country were incomparable.

Today, I am gratefully remembering each and every one of those people who gave me such a wonderful experience in Tokyo.

* * *

59.

A Sustainable Footwear Revolution

Our video content, produced by CAT Productions, has been at the forefront of several successful fundraising campaigns for startups in India and abroad over the past 5-6 years. Recently, a startup co-founder contacted me to discuss a fundraising campaign he was planning. This particular startup and its product were truly impressive. They created shoes and footwear from waste plastic bottles and recycled shoes. Like any other product, sustainable footwear holds great significance in the current global scenario.

The footwear industry produces about 24 billion pairs of shoes each year for nearly 7.8 billion people worldwide, and approximately 400 million pairs are discarded annually, creating vast amounts of waste. Meanwhile, about 4.5 trillion plastic bottles have been produced globally in the last ten years. The scale of these numbers is alarming, and I genuinely feel that the purpose and vision of this startup are commendable. My gratitude goes to the co-founders for their innovative and respectful ideas.

* * *

60.

Sculpting Minimalism: Crafting Beauty In Simplicity

A couple of years ago, I had the opportunity to meet a sculptor in Bangalore and spend quite a bit of time with him. I had always wondered how a sculpture is created. I asked him, "How do you do it?"

He explained that when working with stone, he removes the unwanted parts and reveals the sculpture that was already within the stone. I responded, "Okay." This wasn't a new concept; I had heard it before.

He also shared that, from a very young age, he had a strong inclination towards minimalism, and his minimalist lifestyle was interconnected with his sculptural work. This element was new to me, so I asked, "Why is that?"

He discussed minimalism and mentioned that he owns only 82 possessions. He showed me a list that included his laptop, cellphone, tools, four or five pairs of trousers, shoes, books, a bike, and even a bath towel. Altogether, he possessed only 82 items, which I found fascinating.

One principle of minimalism is that our happiness, joy, and sense of fulfillment are not based on the volume of possessions we have. For example, if you look at your wardrobe, you'll likely find clothes you bought on a whim and haven't worn in months; you probably don't use half of the clothes you own regularly.

The same applies to a house–crockery, gadgets, décor items, books, and even photos in our phone gallery. We often acquire things out of compulsions created by the external world, which can lead to misery.

I have started practicing minimalism, and it has liberated me in many ways. I'm grateful for this beautiful idea! If it resonates with you, consider trying and enjoying a minimalist lifestyle.

* * *

61.

The Empty Pot: A Seeker's Perspective

I still remember an old Zen story. There was a Zen master who admitted only one new disciple every ten years. When the time for new admissions came, he asked the candidates to bring an object that would completely represent a student. From the thousands of candidates, he admitted only one young man who carried an empty pot. Being a disciple means completely surrendering to the master in order to receive wisdom from him.

The mindset of the disciple should be like an empty pot–free of prejudices and preloaded knowledge, embodying true emptiness. Such emptiness can bring wisdom to our hearts. Whenever we assume the role of a disciple, we should empty our minds and receive ideas and perceptions from the master like an empty pot because if the pot is not empty, the wisdom poured in by the master will simply spill out. Today, I extend my gratitude to this humble Zen story.

* * *

62.

Shades Of Blue: Comfort And Joy

I'm not sure if this is true for everyone, but when I check my wardrobe, I notice that the majority of my clothes are in one color–blue or shades of blue. I've loved the color since I was a child. Many times, I've wondered why I lean towards blue shades–perhaps because I love looking at the sky and the ocean. Blue represents vastness; it is serene and evokes possibilities and imagination. These qualities may have inspired my preference for blue, and consciously or unconsciously, I tend to choose it.

The back cover of my cell phone, the shoes I select, the belt I wear–blue appears in many places. It doesn't mean I only choose blue, but the majority of my choices are blue. Some historians claim that ancient civilizations had no color called blue or that there was no word for the color blue. On the other hand, psychology suggests that blue represents conservatives, reliable people, and thinkers who are not impulsive and loyal and who cherish peace and harmony. I don't know whether these traits apply to me or to other blue lovers, but many studies suggest this about those who like blue. Today, I extend my gratitude to this beautiful color, which always brings me comfort, confidence, and happiness.

* * *

63.

The Dance Of Meaningful Coincidences

Today is the 63rd day of gratitude in this series. I use many hashtags, and one of them that I repeatedly use is #Synchronicity. A friend of mine asked me, "What does it mean?" So, I thought I should write about synchronicity.

Synchronicity has its roots in Greek, from *syn* (together) and *chronos* (time). It refers to incidents that happen together with a low probability of occurring simultaneously. For example, when you think about a friend, and he calls you, or when you crave chocolate, and someone shows up with some–these are instances of synchronicity.

In other words, they can be understood as meaningful coincidences. When we pay enough attention to everything that happens in our lives, we can see that a result is the result of many causes. Whenever a significant change occurs in our lives, it becomes easier to decode that event. By paying close attention, we can break down every small occurrence in our lives into its various causes. Synchronicity is a magical formula where many causes combine in a certain way to produce a particular result, which could be positive or negative. If you observe the events that happen to you, you can decode the causes behind them, allowing you to shape your destiny by understanding these reasons and potentially improving your future. Today, I express my gratitude for the phenomenon of synchronicity.

* * *

64.

Mondo Bongo

Today, I felt like talking about one of my favorite songs. It's like summer rain on a warm night! I'm referring to "Mondo Bongo" by Joe Strummer & The Mescaleros from the album *Mondo Bongo.* This song is very special to me. I play it with love–whether I'm driving, watching the rain from the balcony, at private parties, or during many soothing moments, I simply play it! This song is also beautifully featured in the movie *Mr. & Mrs. Smith*, starring Brad Pitt and Angelina Jolie, which is another of my favorite movies. As I write this, the song is playing in the background. I want to express my gratitude to this song and its creators for bringing so much joy to my life!

* * *

65.

You Can Touch The Way 'Deeper'

I recently came across a groundbreaking study on human tactile perception (the sense of touch) by a team of Swedish scientists. The study shows that people can detect differences at the nanoscale while running their fingers over a seemingly smooth surface–up to 13 nanometers!

To put this in perspective, if our fingers were the size of the Earth, we could feel the difference between buildings, trees, and vehicles on the planet. Many of us might overlook our sense of touch, but it is remarkably powerful and sensitive. Let's embrace this awareness and explore the vast possibilities of our tactile perception from this moment on. My gratitude goes to nature, the universe, and evolution for gifting us such an incredible sense of engagement with the physical world!

* * *

66.

Choosing The Five: The Power Of Social Circles

I recently read the famous quote by American entrepreneur and author Jim Rohn: "You are the average of the five people you spend the most time with." I personally love this perspective. It's a sensible framework for self-auditing. If we want to change our position or improve ourselves, we should be mindful of the people we spend time with, as they play crucial roles in shaping our destiny.

This concept is also applicable to our virtual world—whether it's on social media, messengers, or even our call list. We can easily identify the five people with whom we interact the most online, and they will influence us regardless. Moving forward, let's be more discerning about the company we keep. I'm grateful to Jim Rohn for this insightful thought.

* * *

67.

Wabi-Sabi: Embracing Imperfect Perfection

Our choices are often unknowingly dictated by the socio-economic environment we live in. This world demands and imposes a great sense of perfection, symmetry, and proportion that applies to almost everything, from our belongings to our physique. The pursuit of perfection has become a new standard of aesthetics in the modern world.

Recently, I came across a Japanese Buddhist aesthetic (Zen philosophy) called Wabi-Sabi. In short, it is the art of embracing imperfection, acknowledging reality, and being content with originality. I found this concept truly beautiful. In the past, our society had a system where if part of your clothing was torn, it would be stitched and used again—similar to a chappal, bag, or other items.

However, the pursuit of perfection has led people to view such repairs as shameful or a symbol of poverty.

If there is an extra pound of mass on the belly or if the eyebrows are not threaded perfectly, people may see it as a sign of imperfection or failure and feel disheartened. This may stem from idealized mental images influenced by supermodels or certain lifestyles. In contrast, Wabi-Sabi celebrates imperfection, originality, weakness, solitude, asymmetry, roughness, fragility, modesty, and other authentic conditions without judgment, viewing them as exquisite states.

Wabi-Sabi encourages us to be closer to our true selves rather than pretending to be something else. It is an amazing perspective that keeps us grounded and helps us understand who we really are. It allows us to prioritize progress over perfection. Today, I am deeply grateful for this beautiful aesthetic perspective of Wabi-Sabi, which helps us lead an imperfectly perfect life.

* * *

68.

Exascale Computing: Revolutionizing Our Technological Landscape

Today, I read about exascale machines—supercomputers capable of performing at least one quintillion (1,000,000,000,000,000,000) calculations per second. Aurora and Frontier are major exascale machines set to become operational by 2021, developed by Argonne National Laboratory and Oak Ridge National Laboratory. These futuristic computers are expected to tackle numerous challenges, from advanced weather forecasting (involving hundreds of thousands of parameters) to human-computer interaction and personalized medicine. The scope and applications are vast. These exascale computers will transform the way we experience the world in the coming decades. My gratitude goes to the scientists working to make these mammoth machines a reality.

* * *

69.

It's Not Net Sitting Or Net Eating

I was discussing networking today. Networking is an overused and perhaps often abused term these days. Among all the points we discussed, I particularly liked the perspective of Ivan Misner, the founder of BNI, one of the largest networking organizations for business owners.

His idea was: "It is not Net sitting or Net eating; it is Net Working!" It literally blew my mind. Today, I'm extending my gratitude for this amazing perspective!

* * *

70.

Sowing Seeds Of Patience: Lessons From The Farmland

I've often felt that farming is one of the most significant exercises for practicing patience and perseverance. When I was a child, I lived at my ancestral home, where we had paddy fields out front. I wanted my own small paddy area (maybe a couple of square feet) and started sowing rice seeds. I watered them daily, but they didn't grow. Later, one of my uncles discovered that I was pulling them out almost every day to check if they had grown roots. He taught me the lesson of patience for the first time.

We need to tend to everything with care. Farming has a broad spectrum of possibilities–from cultivating relationships to education to wealth! Every abundant harvest is the result of the effort we put into cultivating it, whether we realize it or not. Let's be farmers and plant great seeds for the life we want. My gratitude goes to the magical quality of sensible patience in all of us, which is crucial for nurturing success.

* * *

71.

Timenomics: Maximizing The Value Of Every Second

I read an excerpt from the novel *If Only It Were True* (French: *Et si c'était vrai*) by French novelist Marc Levy. It goes: Imagine you wake up every day with 86,400 dollars in your bank account. By evening, the bank will withdraw any remaining balance, and the next day, it will be filled with another 86,400 dollars. You cannot carry forward any balance to the next day, but you can spend the money each day. You would do everything in your power to spend or invest it wisely because you knew it would be withdrawn forever.

Every day, our lives are filled with 86,400 seconds. Whether we spend or invest them wisely, they cannot be carried forward to the next day. The unspent time is lost forever, and the next day brings another 86,400 seconds. So why waste time and not make the best use of it?

The clock is running. Let's make the most of today's seconds! My gratitude to Marc Levy for this brilliant and invaluable observation!

* * *

72.

Dots: Simplifying Success, One Hour At A Time

I came across the LinkedIn profile of an entrepreneur who was recognized by LinkedIn as one of its 'Top Voices' of 2019. On his profile, I noticed one of his philosophies, or 'codes for life,' called DOTS–Do One Thing Surely!

He suggests that whatever you want to do, pick that one thing and work on it for at least an hour. Don't think about tomorrow or other things you need to do or are missing out on! Just focus on DOTS for one hour a day. No goals or anticipation of results, just pure action! Sooner or later, it will bring you amazing results. I think this is a fantastic approach to try out in life. I have already found my DOTS. My gratitude to the entrepreneur who shared this perspective.

* * *

73.

Cracking The Habit Loop: Insights From The Power Of Habit

I was going through some notes I made after reading the book *The Power of Habit* by Charles Duhigg. He explains that to create and redesign a habit, we need to understand its basic formulation. Every habit loop has three elements: the cue (craving), the routine, and the reward. All these elements are necessary for a habit to work. If a cue is absent, the loop won't complete, and thus the habit won't be formed.

One of the golden rules addressed by the book is this: we cannot eliminate a habit, but we can replace it by maintaining the cue and reward while shifting the routine.

Anytime is the right time to change a habit, and it's a wonderful read for those who wish to experiment with their habits! My gratitude to Charles Duhigg for this insightful book.

* * *

74.

Gut Microbiome: Guardians Of Our Well-Being

I was reading about gut bacteria (the gut microbiome) and their critical role in our well-being. It is estimated that over 100 trillion such bacteria live in our digestive systems, making our lives possible.

In the gut microbiome, the 'good' bacteria primarily help us break down food and turn nutrients into substances our bodies can use. They also help keep the 'bad' bacteria in check by multiplying so often that the unhealthy kind doesn't have space to grow. A healthy balance of bacteria in our gut brings a certain degree of equilibrium to our bodies.

Researchers say that our gut is in constant communication with our brain, and it's possible that the balance of bacteria in the gut microbiome affects our emotions and intellect. It can also influence our instincts and intuitive qualities.

Today, I'm extending my gratitude to the gut microbiome for sustaining our lives.

* * *

75.

Tonality: Enhancing Communication Effectiveness

I was casually surfing online and came across a quote that struck me: "Communication is one thing, but your tone of communication is everything!"

It struck me because it's a universal truth. We are all taught many ways to enhance our ability to communicate in school and college, but the specific tone of communication is equally important.

We all know that sometimes, just the wrong tone can ruin an entire conversation or event! Along with what we communicate, the tone of communication is what makes the effort put into it successful.

I'm extending my gratitude for this amazing perspective today.

* * *

76.

Spreading Smiles

I saw a WhatsApp story from a friend of mine. He had posted, “If I made you smile just once, say hi.”

I paused and sent him a text saying “hi,” and we ended up having a chat.

Wanting to make someone smile or being the humble reason for someone’s smile is truly humane. Let’s pause for a couple of minutes and reflect on the day. and think of the people who made us smile today.

Let’s thank them in our hearts.

* * *

77.

Transforming Should Be Into Musts

One of my favorite topics is the art of execution. I believe every great result we see in personal and professional life, whether in individuals, organizations, or governments, is the result of excellent execution. How people design, prioritize, and execute things shapes the world we experience today.

Executing tasks means prioritizing and scheduling smaller tasks over time toward a common goal, and we experience the art of execution in the big picture. In this context, I recently encountered a perspective from a famous life coach in the United States. He said there's a difference between "should" and "must."

We know there are many things we "should" do to steer our lives in the direction we desire, and we often categorize these tasks as "shoulds" because we recognize their importance.

However, he suggests moving some of these tasks to a category called "must," where they become non-negotiable. The more things we shift from "should" to "must," the more visible progress we will see toward achieving our goals.

Today, I am extending my gratitude to the fantastic life coach who shared this insightful thought with the world.

* * *

78.

Memories Framed: Gratitude For Photographs

Today, I was having a discussion with a friend about our childhood photographs–those from our early years, through school, and the transformations we've undergone over time.

When we consciously review our old photographs, many memories, and events associated with them resurface. It was a wonderful experience for me, taking me back two to three decades–it felt like a form of time travel. The conversation and the photographs were precious.

Let us preserve as many photographs of our past as we can. While we may forget many details, these images serve as valuable tools for reviving memories and making them immortal.

Today, I am extending my gratitude for the photographs I have, which made my day special.

* * *

79.

An Angel On The Highway

A few weeks ago, I was traveling to another city and had parked my car on the side of the road while booking a hotel at night. Unexpectedly, a bike rider hit my car.

I saw him being flung off the bike and crashing down. I thought he was dead. Lots of people ran to him and gathered around. I panicked because of the crowd, the guy lying on the road with his broken bike and helmet, and the fact that the back of my car was almost completely wrecked. People started discussing whose fault it was and similar matters. Later, we realized that the rider was drunk. It was a serious situation, and I didn't know how to handle it.

Suddenly, a person appeared. He started talking to me, trying to understand what had happened, and spoke to the local people to calm them down. He checked the bike rider, made sure he wasn't seriously injured, gave him water, made him comfortable, and asked me to contact the nearest police station. He provided me with the phone number to report the incident. Then he noticed the rider was drunk and didn't want him to get into trouble, so he asked if I had insurance for my car, and I confirmed that I did.

He advised me that when the police arrived, I should tell them I'd settle the case between the bike rider and myself without legal complexities. He even helped me tie up the rear bumper, which was falling down. He resolved the situation with ease and then disappeared.

Someone from nowhere appeared, helped me, did his job, and vanished without waiting for acknowledgement or even a word of thanks. What should I call this phenomenon? Some people seem like illusions–they appear out of nowhere, fulfill their purpose in our lives, and disappear without any expectation of recognition.

Today, I am gratefully remembering the divine being who appeared and helped me at midnight on the National Highway.

* * *

80.

Discerning Love: What It Is And Isn't

There is a vast amount of literature in numerous forms and languages that glorifies love. I felt it was important to share what I believe love is not:

- If something limits you or holds you back, it is not love.

- If there is bloodshed involved for any reason, it cannot be love.

- If you've been taught that tears embellish love, that's not true–tears do not define love.

- If something suffocates you or makes you feel insecure, it's not love.

- If you believe that great sacrifices glorify love, that's not true.

- If something reduces your productivity or distracts you from your focus, it's not love.

- If anything triggers the worst in you, it is certainly not love.

- If you ever have to pretend, it's not love.

- If it makes you suffer, it cannot be love. And if the feeling doesn't transform you into a better human being, it can never be love.

As we approach Valentine's Day tomorrow, let's be grateful for all the love we have experienced and maintain a clear perspective on what love truly is and what it is not.

* * *

81.

Leadership In Adversity: Embracing Failure With Responsibility

Recently, I watched a video of Dr. APJ Abdul Kalam, our former president and "The Missile Man." In the video, he recounted his experience during the launch of the SLV-3 (satellite launch vehicle) in 1979. He was the mission director for this experimental launch, which took place at the launching pad in Sriharikota. The mission, the result of the effort of thousands of people over more than 10 years, was crucial to him, so he was understandably nervous.

Just before the launch, he received a warning from the computer that the system was not fit for launch due to an error in the control system. Despite the warning, he decided to proceed with the launch. Unfortunately, the mission failed, and the SLV crashed into the Bay of Bengal instead of reaching orbit.

Feeling panicked and depressed, Dr. Kalam was accompanied by his senior officer, Prof. Satish Dhawan, to a press conference where the media were waiting. The media criticized him harshly for the loss of money and resources. Prof. Satish Dhawan addressed the media, saying, "Friends, we failed this time, and we will try our best to succeed in our next attempt." He took full responsibility for the failure upon himself.

The following year, in 1980, Dr. Kalam addressed the vulnerabilities and successfully launched the SLV into orbit. This time, Prof. Satish Dhawan asked Dr. Kalam to lead the press conference and address the media, which earned him much applause.

In the video, Dr. Kalam highlighted the remarkable qualities of a leader who willingly embraces failure and takes responsibility when things go wrong. When they succeed, they joyfully share the fruits of success with their team. This is a valuable lesson, and I believe such leaders make the world a better place.

Today, let's be grateful to such leaders who have improved our lives. Let us also strive to embody these leadership qualities in our own lives.

* * *

82.

Heartfelt Correction: A Grateful Remembrance

A few years ago, I was invited to an engineering college in Tamil Nadu to deliver a session on the adventurous journey of entrepreneurship. There was a crowd of over 500 students who were kind and patient enough to listen to my talk. I spoke for an hour or more, including an interactive session with them.

One of the key mantras I shared was, "Listen Your Heart" and make choices accordingly, as I truly believe that no one knows us better than our hearts. The students were engaged, entertained, and hopefully inspired. After the session, the management was happy, and the HOD was satisfied. As I was leaving the stage to go to the principal's office, a faculty member gently approached me and said, "Mr. Amarnath, ethum thappa ninachidathinge (please don't feel bad), I have to tell you something."

I was in the middle of a crowd of students, teachers, and many others. From his gesture, I understood that he wanted to speak to me personally. I took him aside and asked, "What happened, sir?"

He replied, "Amarnath, I am a member of the English faculty at this college."

I responded, "Okay."

He continued, "I liked your session very much, but if you say 'Listen to your Heart,' it would be better and more accurate. I thought I should mention this to you."

It was then that I realized that, although I meant to say 'Listen to your Heart,' I had missed adding the 'to' multiple times during my session. I took his hands, thanked him deeply, and said, "Sir, thank you so much for pointing out the mistake I made." Perhaps that day, beyond everything, his genuine comment touched my heart.

In life, there will be people who applaud us or pretend to applaud us for whatever we do. We need to recognize and understand them, but what we truly need are people who want us to excel and who are brave enough to point out and correct our mistakes.

Today, I wholeheartedly and gratefully remember the faculty member from that college who corrected me to "listen to my heart."

* * *

83.

Seeds Of Devil And Divine

There is always a seed of the devil and the divine inside every person. What I feel is that a person turns into either a devil or a divine being based on how we nurture that seed in them. In short, we are responsible for the divinity or devilishness a person shows towards us.

Let us figure out, water, and nurture the divine seed in others! I'm grateful for this awesome thought that popped into my mind during a conversation with a friend one morning.

* * *

84.

Guarding Dignity: Stories Behind The Uniform

There used to be a security guard at our apartment whom I remember well because, whenever we met in the morning, he would pleasantly say, “Good morning.” It wasn’t just a formality; it was genuinely pleasant.

We rarely interact with security guards—they open our gate and close it. I would usually speak with him when I had to pick up an online delivery or a courier. After he learned that I am an entrepreneur, he would discuss business and the recession, showing a keen interest in these topics. One day, while I was collecting an Amazon package, he asked me about the possibility of an IPO (public listing of an organization). It wasn’t something typically expected from a security guard, so

I asked him, "Are you very interested in these things? What makes you talk about this?"

He then revealed his story: he had been a general manager working for a manufacturing company owned by the royal family in Muscat, Oman, in the early '90s. Later, he built his own logistics company and expanded it from Muscat to the UAE with over 150 employees. He also entered the construction business. During the 2008 recession, he purchased materials from China, but due to diplomatic issues between Oman and China, the shipment didn't reach Muscat, and he ran out of cash.

At that time, his business couldn't recover as planned. His cash flow was affected, and he had to shut down the company and sell all his properties. Despite losing all his wealth, his home, and his health, he ensured he settled payments to all his employees. And now he was a security guard.

In a world where businessmen often escape with billions of dollars, a noble man like him, who paid all his employees, is now a gatekeeper. I have great respect for him.

In our lives, whether in a hotel, apartment, shopping mall, or ATM kiosk, security guards and people who open and close doors for us often have incredible stories that make them who they are. So, today, let's remember them with gratitude and respect.

* * *

85.

A Cosmic Response

This happened while I was in college. I studied at a college in Tamil Nadu, in a remote village called Kalayarkoil near Madurai. I had to stay behind after all my friends had left since I had failed a paper and needed to retake the exam. The paper was called English Communication. In the history of the college, only three or four people had failed it because it was meant to be an easy paper, but I had failed that subject multiple times.

I was staying in a room outside the campus. It was a remote village, and restaurants were temporarily shut down when students went home. So, at that time, there were no restaurants, and I had to go to the nearest town for food.

On that day, I couldn't go to town because I was working on something and forgot about food. It was only around 10 p.m. that I realized how late it was. There were no buses or any other transportation after 10. In the morning, I had eaten biscuits and had skipped lunch. At night, I was alone, and it was a horrible feeling. I was extremely hungry.

Around 2 a.m., I heard the sound of a truck approaching the place where I was staying, and two people came out of the truck. I was afraid because it was very late, I was alone, and these were two strangers in an unknown place. One of them came to me and asked, "Can we have some water?" I said, "Okay, brother," gave him water, and as they were about to leave, he returned and asked if they could sit and have their dinner here. I told him to feel free; I had no problem with that. He then asked if I had had my dinner, and I told him, "Yes, I did, around 10 o'clock," but he insisted that I join them. I initially refused, but he kept insisting, saying it was okay to have food. So I joined them–the driver and his cleaner/assistant. We sat around the food, and they shared dosa, sambar, and omelet with me that night.

I think that dinner tasted more delicious than any five-course meal I have ever had in my life.

What I'm saying is that sometimes when your heart sends a genuine call, the universe responds, and it responds in an amazing way. I've been lucky enough to have had many experiences like this.

Today, I am grateful to the universe for aligning in a way that is beneficial and merciful to us.

* * *

86.

The Journey Vs. Destination

Whenever we plan something, choosing the ways to reach a destination and the mode of operations, we have to make a decision: focus on the journey or the destination. Often, the choices for both contradict each other in terms of comfort and involvement.

This is an age-old debate–whether to focus on the journey or the destination–and I was quite curious to know the answer. Whenever I discuss it with my friends, some say they are more focused on the destination, while others focus on the journey. But when I looked within myself, I realized that I am more aligned with focusing on the journey than the destination.

I truly believe that to enjoy traveling, we need to focus on the journey because reaching the destination is a matter of a few moments, while the rest of the effort and experience is the journey itself!

I think the role of the destination is pure inspiration—something that constantly motivates us to be consistent and focused on our journey. We can even break down the journey into small destinations or milestones. I've always felt that when we achieve these one after the other, we get a sense of accomplishment, which triggers happy hormones and helps us move forward in our pursuit of the final destination.

I am gratefully remembering a friend who, a few years ago, opened my mind to this and helped me differentiate between the significance of the journey and the destination.

I'm eager to know your thoughts as well. Do you care more about your journey or your destination? Let me know your choice.

* * *

87.

For All Unknown Singers

I was having dinner with my friends at a restaurant. There were very few people, probably because of the COVID-19 scenario, but there was well-maintained social distancing and other safety measures.

There was a singer performing for the guests. Even though I was chatting with my friends, I kept observing him. People were coming and going, laughing, and celebrating a birthday, but he kept singing song after song. Some people greeted him, some appreciated him, and some didn't even notice him, but he continued to sing.

I felt that he was doing a great job, maintaining his performance regardless of his audience or whether people appreciated him. He might have been doing this for days or years–singing in the restaurant without concern for external validation. He performed well and was completely detached from the appreciation of those listening.

I think it is wonderful to express our gratitude to all the singers who serenade us melodiously, making our moments more beautiful, even though we might sometimes ignore or overlook them.

* * *

88.

The Art Of Introspection

Introspection is one of the key ways to elevate ourselves from good to better, and ultimately to the best. I am a die-hard fan of the process of self-examination–looking into ourselves in all aspects: from the physical to our persona, to our character, to our basic instincts and longings, and to the many deep layers within us. This process begins with the physical, the outer layer of our being, and the best way to approach it is by looking in the mirror.

I don't know how many of you have seriously looked into mirrors!

Mirrors are mysterious objects.

Instead of just casually glancing at yourself in the mirror before heading out, take some time to look at yourself for an extended period of time. A lot of things about yourself will be revealed in front of you!

It's an experience you should try. It shouldn't be a one-time occurrence but a continuous process. Day after day, spend time looking in mirrors for a while. Just be with your own reflection; it's an incredible experience.

I highly recommend trying this process. It will help you learn more about yourself and make you appreciate yourself more.

Today, I am extending my gratitude to the thought leaders who, years ago, truly inspired me to take the process of introspection seriously.

* * *

89.

The Power Of Follow-Up

A new entrepreneur recently discussed his business with me. I asked how things were going, and he mentioned that while things were good, the main challenge was maintaining cash flow. Even though projects were being delivered, it was hard to get clients to make payments.

I asked if he followed up with them, and he said yes. He mentioned that he sent an email and waited a week before sending another. When I asked if he called or texted them, he said he called once every 5 to 7 days, even after delivering the product.

I told him that approach was ineffective. I had been in his position years ago and had hesitated as well, but I realized something: we live in a world of distractions. Even if a client or vendor genuinely wants to pay, they might forget or prioritize other things in this ocean of distractions.

Follow-ups at intervals of 5 to 7 days will not work in this era of information overload. Whether it's a payment, reply, call, or answer, everyone is immersed in an ocean of information and priorities. The only solution is constant, persistent follow-up.

Even I tell people that I will do something for them and ask them to remind me because I forget. We handle many tasks daily, so it's easy to forget.

So that's the key–follow up relentlessly. Trust me, you will see the results. That's my word.

Today, I am gratefully remembering a senior entrepreneur who shared the power of follow-up with me in the early days when I started my enterprise.

* * *

90.

Kindness Brewed With Tea

This evening, as I was driving back to my apartment, I felt like having tea. I parked my car near a small tea shop, which was quite crowded both inside and outside. I felt a bit lazy about going out and waiting for my tea, so I was considering what to do.

I noticed a guy from the tea shop approach a car parked in front of mine. He spoke to the passengers inside and then went back to the tea shop. After a while, he returned with tea and snacks for them. I honked and waved to get his attention. He came over, I gave him money, and I ordered tea and a banana fry. He looked at me for a moment and then went back to the shop.

A minute later, he returned with tea and a freshly made banana fry wrapped in tissue paper, and he gave me my change. I enjoyed the crunchy, sweet banana fry with the wonderful tea; it was a calm and positive Sunday evening.

After some time, I saw the tea seller get into the driver's seat of the car in front of me and drive away with a smile on his face. I was shocked. I had thought he was a worker at the tea shop, which is why I had called him over and placed my order. I didn't realize he was the driver of the car.

I didn't know what to say about this person. I didn't know his name or who he was, but I was convinced he was a great soul. Today, I am gratefully remembering this stranger who served me my evening tea.

* * *

91.

Tale Of Sudhakaran: The Luckseller

Recently, I read a news report about a story from Kanhangad, a town in northern Kerala.

There was a person named Sudhakaran who ran a small shop selling sweets, juice, cold drinks, and lottery tickets. One day, one of his regular customers, Ashokan, asked him to set aside ten lottery tickets for him. Ashokan then forgot about it.

Later, Sudhakaran discovered that one of the tickets he had set aside for Ashokan had won the first prize, amounting to about 10 million Indian rupees. Ashokan had not paid for the tickets, nor had Sudhakaran informed him that he had set them aside.

Despite this, Sudhakaran called Ashokan and told him that one of the tickets he had set aside had won the first prize. He could have kept the ticket for himself and claimed the money, but he chose not to. He wasn't wealthy and wasn't free of financial liabilities, but he still made the call.

Some people are like that; to act as Sudhakaran did requires a great deal of strength and integrity. His act humbles me and makes me reflect on the concept of righteousness. People like Sudhakaran are very rare on this planet.

Today, with much respect, I am gratefully remembering Sudhakaran's divine act.

* * *

92.

Decisive Whispers: Your Body's Guidance

One of the constantly evolving challenges we face as humans is decision-making. Every day, we make countless decisions–small and large. When it comes to making crucial decisions and you're unsure how to proceed logically or what to choose, there's a solution in a technique introduced to me by one of my mentors.

You make yourself available to or imagine yourself in one of the choices, believing you are with that option. If you don't feel a clear logical or emotional response, listen to and observe your body. Imagine yourself in each situation presented by your choices, and note how your body reacts to them. You can understand your body's response and choose the option with which your body feels most comfortable. This method goes beyond logical reasoning and emotional influences.

Your body is a result of millions of years of evolution, and it can communicate insights beyond the intelligence you have acquired in your lifetime.

Listen to your body and make the right choice. All the very best.

Today, I am gratefully remembering the person who introduced me to this fantastic technique.

* * *

93.

The Procrastination Puzzle: Unraveling Its Psychology

I recently listened to a podcast about procrastination—why people procrastinate and the psychology behind postponing tasks.

In essence, the podcast explains that procrastination often occurs because you don't really want to do something; you do it because it is required for another purpose. You might complete a task to gain something, which in turn leads to further rewards. The initial steps might be tedious and unappealing, but they are part of a larger goal.

The idea to combat procrastination is straightforward: focus on tasks you genuinely want to do. If you continuously procrastinate, examine why you are avoiding the task and whether you truly want to do it, or if something else is more engaging.

Procrastination is a topic that has been discussed extensively, but it remains relevant because it affects our quality of life and productivity.

Today, I am extending my gratitude to the master who shared his wisdom through that podcast.

* * *

94.

Mocha: A Journey From Port To Palate

A friend of mine was discussing his idea for a coffee business, from procurement to flavors and selling the product entirely online. I listened keenly; his dream was quite interesting. He then asked me, "Do you know when we started drinking coffee, especially Indians?"

I thought maybe, like pepper, it was always present in the Western Ghats and had been used for centuries. But he told me I was wrong and enlightened me with some fascinating facts about coffee that were completely new to me.

The concept of coffee as a drink originated in Yemen in the middle of the 15th century. The original Arabic word for coffee was "Qahwah" (meaning appetite suppressant). There was a port named Mocha, which was very famous for trade at that time, and through this port, coffee became known to the outside world. "Qahwah" turned into "kahve" in Turkish, "koffie" in Dutch, and "coffee" in English.

Interestingly, there was a Sufi in South India named Baba Budan. In the 16th century, on his return from a pilgrimage to Mecca via Yemen, he collected seven coffee beans from the Yemeni port of Mocha. These beans became the very first coffee seeds ever grown in South India. Baba Budan was from Chikmagalur in Karnataka, and later, India became one of the largest coffee exporters in history.

That was quite surprising to me. Even the word "mocha," which I thought was just another Italian term like caffè latte, was actually the name of a Yemeni port. It was an eye-opening discussion, and I thought I should share this with you.

Today, I am gratefully remembering Baba Budan for bringing those coffee beans to India, which turned into a favorite drink for many of us.

* * *

95.

Transistors: The Invisible Architects Of The Digital Age

We are living in a time of digital transcendence, paving the way for Industry 4.0, the next level of machine learning and artificial intelligence systems. Whether it's your cell phone, laptop, or the digital systems in your car, the core factor that makes all these technologies possible is the microprocessor. Essentially, the "computer" in every device we use is the microprocessor, the core of every digital system. Every microprocessor is fundamentally based on transistors, a phenomenal invention.

Recently, I watched a documentary on the evolution of transistors, and it blew my mind. The size of a transistor we now use is ten thousand times smaller than a strand of hair, and inside a microprocessor, there are about three hundred million transistors functioning on average.

Transistors control the flow of electrons in a microprocessor with their switching and amplification functions, making the entire computer operational. If a microprocessor is the brain of a computer, then transistors are the brain cells within it. I don't know how many of us are aware of transistors; they were invented in the mid-20th century and won a Nobel Prize in 1947. This invention played a pivotal role in modern computing.

Today, I am gratefully remembering the widely overlooked fundamental component of all our computer systems, including mobile phones, laptops, and wearable devices like fitness bands–the transistor!

* * *

96.

The Witness State: Navigating Life's Unfolding Journey

From the 20th century onward, art forms, especially films across languages, have typically featured a hero who encounters a problem. The hero gets involved in the issue, sometimes even when it's not his business. He engages with it, makes his life difficult, makes many sacrifices, and experiences fights, love, vengeance, victory, and revenge. This formula for a popular movie is consistent across languages.

Generations, including mine, have grown up with the subconscious understanding that being a hero in life means finding and solving problems. However, this perspective is misguided. In reality, there are very few problems and challenges that require our active response. Many issues resolve themselves naturally in our absence; what we truly need is the perspective of a witness.

This is a beautiful way to view the world. Whether you are at a function, a shopping mall, a theater, a crowd, a restaurant, or even on the street, it is enlightening to observe and witness what is happening without interacting with those occurrences. It's something that must be experienced to be fully understood.

Observe people and things around you and notice what's happening. There will be events that make you happy and others that make you sad. Rather than engaging with them, simply witness them, and you'll find that many problems will eventually resolve on their own.

If you feel that a situation genuinely calls for your involvement and you have a role to play, then engage with it. Otherwise, stand back and observe.

Today, I am gratefully remembering Osho Rajneesh, who had many reflections on this concept of witnessing. What I have mentioned here is just the first layer of witnessing; there are many deeper layers, and I look forward to sharing those perspectives another day.

* * *

97.
Night Owl Reflections

Of course, I can wake up early when there are specific requirements, but in general, I am more of a night owl than an early bird. I believe I've followed the same sleep cycle for the past 15 years.

Many people have asked me why I stay up so late and what keeps me awake through the night. The truth is simple: as night approaches, I often feel a sense of not having accomplished enough, or I feel that I could be doing more. This drives me to continue working—whether researching, reading, watching infotainment content, or writing. I keep at it until I achieve a sense of satisfaction or a feeling of productivity, and only then do I go to sleep.

I think every night owl has their own justification or reason for staying up late. For me, there is a subtle driving force inspired by one of my favorite poems by Robert Frost, "Stopping by Woods on a Snowy Evening," particularly its final stanza:

"The woods are lovely, dark, and deep,
But I have promises to keep,
and miles to go before I sleep."

These lines have profoundly influenced me, encouraging me to keep moving forward and achieving more before I sleep.

Today, I am gratefully remembering this beautiful poem by Robert Frost.

* * *

98.

Only This Will Lead You To That

Jalal ad-Din Muhammed Rumi was a 13th-century Persian scholar, poet, and Sufi mystic who transcended the life and customs of his time.

Rumi's thoughts, perceptions, and poetry are timeless—they are relevant today and will continue to be in the future, I hope. They are universal, filled with love, compassion, gratitude, devotion, humility, simplicity, beauty, and many other qualities that can strengthen our spirit.

Recently, I came across a note with a couple of lines from Rumi:

I asked, "Why have I received only this?"
A voice replied, "Only this will lead you to that."

I find this perspective remarkable. Rumi has distilled the mystery, sorrow, complexity, and unpredictability of life into these two sentences. When faced with difficulty or uncertainty, people often ask, "Why have I received this?"

Rumi suggests that "only this can lead you to that," opening up endless possibilities.

My conviction is that these two sentences are enough to help anyone on this planet survive and excel in any aspect of life.

Today, I am gratefully remembering these lines from the great Jalal ad-Din Muhammed Rumi.

* * *

99.

When They Go Low, We Go High

Last week, a friend of mine called me because he had a disagreement with another person who began sharing derogatory information about him on social media and engaging in cyberbullying.

My friend asked if he should retaliate, as he knew some vulnerable points about the other person. He approached me because, many years ago, I was professionally associated with official departments that handle cyber disputes in this country.

When hc asked this, my initial reaction was to advise him to retaliate, especially since it was a situation affecting my friend. However, I shared a video of the second presidential debate from 2016 between Donald Trump and Hillary Clinton with him.

In that debate, Trump attempted to undermine Clinton by bringing up the Bill Clinton scandal. This moment was embarrassing for Trump, but Hillary Clinton responded gracefully by quoting Michelle Obama's famous statement: "When they go low, we go high."

My friend watched the video and understood the message I was trying to convey. He decided not to retaliate with cyberbullying but instead formally issued a complaint to the concerned department. He followed through, and the issue was later resolved.

I am a big fan of this powerful principle, and it truly works. I am grateful for the idea that "when they go low, we go high."

* * *

100.
The Power Of Gratitude

I'm sure all of us who read this post are alive right now. Being alive means we are full of life! And life is full of possibilities.

The state of being alive–the ability to breathe, walk on this planet, have a meal, be surrounded by family or friends, use a smartphone and the internet, and the ability to read, write, hear, speak, and smell–already gifts us with abundance!

When I noticed many of my dear ones complaining about their lives and living miserably, forgetting the gifts they have, it made me think about communicating and spreading awareness of the gifts in our lives and the power of gratitude.

The state of being grateful is one of the most profound human qualities, and I have always been 100% certain of its power.

Throughout these 365 days, my conviction about this power was tested daily. Like many of you, I'm also a vulnerable person with less discipline and have never been a "writer" or a "hustler." However, my belief in the power of gratitude remained unshakable because I am deeply grateful for the life I have. Every day, I felt it was my duty to make gratitude shine through in my journey.

Today, I bow to the power of gratitude for helping me complete this 365-day journey of thankfulness! I remember each and every person and factor that made this possible.

I'm so grateful to all of you and everything that keeps me alive!

Thank you!

* * *

REFLECTIONS

1. The Tale Of The Srk Of Jaipur

Self-Reflection: Reflect on the value of literacy and education in your life. How has your ability to read and write shaped your experiences and opportunities? Are there instances where you've witnessed the impact of illiteracy on individuals, similar to the salesman in the story? Jot down the people/institutions that empowered your ability to read and write, and express gratitude for their contributions.

2. Synaptic Symphony: The Orchestra Of Life

Self-Reflection: Reflect on the incredible complexity and importance of neurons and synapses in your body. How does this knowledge change your perspective on the experiences and sensations you have in life? Can you think of ways to better appreciate and care for your brain health? Consider expressing gratitude for the intricate workings of your brain that enable your existence and experiences.

3. Pale Blue Dot: Cosmic Perspective

Self-Reflection: Reflect on the humbling perspective offered by Carl Sagan's description of Earth as a pale blue dot in the vast cosmos. How does this perspective change the way you view your life and the world? Can it help you prioritize what truly matters in the grand scheme of things? Consider expressing gratitude for the opportunity to exist on this tiny speck in the universe and the chance to make a positive impact during your time here. Now, take a moment to jot down your thoughts and feelings inspired by this profound perspective.

4. Gutenberg's Legacy: The Printing Revolution Reimagined

Self-Reflection: Reflect on the impact of Johannes Gutenberg's invention of the mechanical printing technology on the world and the subsequent printing revolution. How has access to books and printed materials shaped your life and knowledge? Can you imagine a world without the printing press and its profound influence on learning and knowledge dissemination? Take a moment to jot down your thoughts and express gratitude for the revolutionary innovation that has enriched our lives for centuries.

5. Water: The New Gold

Self-Reflection: Reflect on the importance of water in your life and the world. How often do you take access to clean and consumable water for granted? Are you conscious of your water consumption and its impact on the environment? Given the increasing scarcity of fresh water in many parts of the world, how can you contribute to water conservation efforts? Take a moment to jot down your thoughts and express gratitude for the privilege of easy access to clean water while considering the global water crisis.

6. Half-Hearted Encore: Lessons From The Stage

Self-Reflection: Reflect on the lesson learned from the experience of performing a drama both wholeheartedly and half-heartedly. Have there been instances in your life where you've approached a task or responsibility with a lack of enthusiasm or commitment? What were the outcomes in those situations? How can you apply the lesson of giving your full effort and commitment to your current endeavors? Jot down your thoughts and express gratitude for the valuable lesson.

7. Unleashing Strengths: Insights From The Iliad

Self-Reflection: Reflect on the concept of recognizing and unleashing one's core strengths and abilities. Have you ever felt pressured to control or suppress your innate talents or instincts due to external influences? How can you identify and embrace your core competencies to achieve your goals and make a positive impact in your life and the lives of others? Jot down your thoughts and express gratitude for the valuable lesson from the story.

8. A Productive Tip From The Interview

Self-Reflection: Reflect on the lesson learned from the story about creating a professional mindset for increased productivity. Have you ever underestimated the impact of dressing professionally, even in a remote or telephonic work setting? How do small changes in your environment or attire affect your work ethic and mindset? Consider the power of subconscious cues in improving productivity and jot down your thoughts. Express gratitude for the valuable lesson from this story.

9. Victory From Within: Sun Tzu's Winning Attitude

Self-Reflection: Reflect on the wisdom of Sun Tzu's quote, "Victorious warriors win first and then go to war, while defeated warriors go to war first and then seek to win." How can this perspective be applied to your life, whether in personal goals or professional endeavors? Have you experienced the difference in outcomes when you approach challenges with a winning attitude versus a defeated mindset? Share your thoughts and express gratitude for this groundbreaking perspective.

10. The Blue And Red Letters

Self Reflection: Reflect on the freedoms you experience today that many in the past lacked. Have you ever taken these liberties for granted? Take a moment to express gratitude for the freedom we enjoy, appreciating the sacrifices made by those before us.

11. A Reflection On Raman Naik's Story

Self-Reflection: Reflect on the experience of witnessing the hotel staff's use of leftovers and their reliance on such food. How does this experience make you feel about the abundance of food in your life? Have you ever been in a situation where you had to make the most of limited resources? How can you appreciate and reduce food wastage in your own life? Express gratitude for the meals you have and the privilege of not experiencing hunger.

12. Nobody Was Ever Thinking About You

Self Reflection: Reflect on how often the fear of others' opinions has held you back from pursuing your dreams or taking bold steps. Have you ever realized, like in Elizabeth Gilbert's insight, that people are more focused on their own lives than on yours? Take a moment to express gratitude for the freedom to live authentically, without the weight of others' perceptions.

13. The Eternal Breath: A Grateful Reflection

Self-Reflection: Take a moment to focus on your breath. How often do you pause to appreciate the simple act of breathing? Reflect on the significance of your breath as the constant companion throughout your life's journey. How can a mindful awareness of your breath bring more gratitude into your daily life?

14. Forgiveness: A Divine Path

Self-Reflection: Reflect on the power of forgiveness and the impact it can have on your life and relationships. Are there any situations or individuals that come to mind where forgiveness could play a positive role? Embracing forgiveness improves your own well-being and the well-being of those around you. Recall the people who have forgiven you... Recall the faces whom you may forgive, jot down their names, and move on.

15. Home: A Sheltering Reminder

Self-Reflection: Take a moment to appreciate the privilege of having a home. Reflect on how it feels to have a place to rest and find comfort. Are there any ways you can contribute to helping those who are homeless or less fortunate to find shelter and support?

16. Silent Blossoms: Unsung Heroes Of Cleanliness

Self-Reflection: Take a moment to appreciate the work of janitors and housekeeping staff who clean up after us, often going unnoticed. Reflect on how you can show appreciation for their hard work and contribute to making their jobs easier. How can you be more considerate in public restrooms and other places you use with more gratitude? Jot down your points.

17. Unbreakable Spirit: Lessons From Louis Zamperini

Self-Reflection: Reflect on the incredible survival instinct and resilience demonstrated by Louis Zamperini during his harrowing ordeal. How does his story inspire you to tap into your own inner strength and face challenges with determination and courage? Consider situations in your life where this spirit of survival has helped you overcome adversity.

18. Candles That Illuminate The Lives Of Others

Self-Reflection: Reflect on the Uber driver's story of sacrifice and determination to support his family's education and well-being. How does his selflessness inspire you to appreciate the sacrifices made by your loved ones? Take a moment to express your gratitude for their efforts and sacrifices in your own life.

19. Echoes Of Yesterdays: Embracing The Sum Of Our Past

Self-Reflection: Reflect on the quote, "Today is the Sum Of all Yesterdays," and its significance in your life. How does acknowledging the role of your past experiences shape your perspective on the present moment? Take a moment to express gratitude for the collection of moments and experiences that have led you to where you are today.

20. The Legacy Of Sir Nicholas Winton

Self-Reflection: Reflect on the remarkable story of Sir Nicholas Winton and his selfless actions to save lives during World War II. How does this story inspire you to think about your own potential to make a positive impact on the world? Consider the profound effect one individual's actions can have on the lives of many.

21. Travel That Unlocks Change

Self-Reflection: Reflect on the role of travel as a tool for personal growth and change, which involves not only moving around places but also exploring people, perspectives, and various aspects of life. How has this holistic approach to travel impacted your life, and what changes or insights have you gained from exploring new people, perspectives, and experiences during your journeys? Consider the value of stepping outside of your comfort zone and embracing new dimensions of life through travel.

22. Diversify Your Investments: Eggs And Baskets

Self-Reflection: Jot down your thoughts and express your gratitude for the valuable advice of not putting all your eggs in one basket. How can this principle apply to different aspects of your life, such as career, investments, personal relationships, and personal growth? Reflect on how diversifying your efforts and investments can lead to a more balanced and secure life.

23. Surrender: Guiding You Through Unknown Chapters

Self-Reflection: Reflect on the concept of surrender and how it applies to your life. Have you ever experienced the power of surrendering to something beyond yourself? How has surrendering influenced your decision-making and the outcomes in your life? Express your gratitude for the guidance and wisdom that led you to understand the importance of surrendering.

24. Inspiration Everywhere: Finding Motivation In The World Around Us

Self-Reflection: Reflect on the sources of inspiration in your life. Do you find inspiration in everyday things and the world around you, or do you actively seek it out? How has inspiration influenced your actions and decisions? Take a moment to express gratitude for the people or things that have inspired you to strive for greatness.

25. Rich Dad Poor Dad

Self-Reflection: Reflect on the impact of a book or piece of literature in your life. How has it shaped your perspective or understanding of certain concepts? What lessons have you taken from it, and how has it influenced your journey?

26. True Richness: Beyond The Illusion Of Wealth

Self-Reflection: Reflect on the concept of true richness. Are there areas of your life where you may have been pretending to be rich or successful to impress others? How can you shift your focus towards pursuing genuine richness in various aspects of your life? Express gratitude for the realization and commitment to true richness.

27. The Temple Of The Heart

Self-Reflection: Reflect on the importance of empathy and having a compassionate heart. How can you cultivate empathy in your own life, and what positive changes can it bring to your interactions with others and the world around you? Express gratitude for the valuable lesson on empathy.

28. The Mystery Of 'Empty Eye'

Self-Reflection: Reflect on the challenges and misunderstandings caused by language and communication barriers. How can we be more empathetic and understanding when dealing with such situations, both as speakers and listeners? Express gratitude for those who have helped clarify misunderstandings and improve communication.

29. No Half Measures, Period.

Self-Reflection: Reflect on your experiences with implementing new systems or policies, and consider how commitment and strict adherence to change can impact success. Are there instances where a lack of commitment hindered progress? Express gratitude for the lessons learned from these experiences.

30. An Unforgettable Meal From An Angel In The Skies

Self-Reflection: Reflect on the kindness and generosity of the cabin crew member who gave her meal to the author. Have you ever given away your meal to anyone unconditionally? If yes, then tap yourself on the shoulder, acknowledge, and appreciate yourself. Recall the people who shared their meals with you. Recall the places where you created touching memories with a meal. Jot them down with gratitude. Remember, there are millions of lives in the world who go to sleep with an empty stomach.

31. Be Intentionally Deaf When You Move Forward

Self-Reflection: Reflect on the concept of being intentionally deaf while driving towards your goal. How can this concept be applied in your life? Are there instances where you've allowed distractions or negative influences to deter you from your goals? How can you be more intentional and focused on your path to success? Additionally, express gratitude for the insights gained from this concept.

32. Simply Vanilla

Self-Reflection: Reflect on your favorite flavor and what it means to you. Is there a deeper connection or sentiment associated with this flavor? How does your preference for this flavor reflect your personality or life experiences? Consider sharing your favorite flavors and the memories or emotions they evoke. Express gratitude for the simple joys that flavors bring to life.

33. Fashion Model

Self-Reflection: Reflect on a time when you made a decision that may have seemed tough or unconventional but ultimately had a positive impact on someone's life. How did that decision align with your values or intuition? Have you ever experienced a similar situation where someone's well-being or happiness was more important than their current role or job? Share your thoughts and express gratitude for the ability to make decisions that positively influence others' paths in life.

34. A Spoonful Of Kindness: A Sweet Childhood Memory

Self-Reflection: Reflect on a time when someone's small act of kindness made a significant impact on your day or life. How did their empathy and generosity affect you? Have you ever had the opportunity to pay it forward by helping someone in a similar way? Share your thoughts and express gratitude for the kindness you've experienced in your life.

35. A Gamble Wheel On The Question Paper

Self-Reflection: Reflect on a time when you misunderstood a concept or instruction, leading to unexpected results or consequences. How did this misunderstanding impact your actions or decisions? What did you learn from the experience, and how has it influenced your approach to understanding instructions or concepts in the future? Share your thoughts and express gratitude for the lessons learned from such experiences.

36. Being In The Flow Of Life

Self Reflection: Reflect on the two approaches to life—crafting it like an architect or letting things flow like a poet or mystic. Have you ever embraced the flow of life rather than trying to control every aspect? How can you strike a balance between actively shaping your life and allowing things to unfold naturally? Take a moment to express gratitude for the choice to live in harmony with life's flow.

37. Curiosity And The Rewarding Circuit In The Brain

Self-Reflection: Reflect on the role of curiosity in your life. Have you noticed moments when your curiosity led you to discover something new or solve a problem? Are there areas of your life where you've become less curious over time? How can you nurture and embrace your sense of curiosity with gratitude to make your life more exciting and fulfilling?

38. Understanding Loss Aversion

Self Reflection: Reflect on the concept of loss aversion and how it affects your own decision-making, especially in areas like finance and purchases. Have you ever noticed yourself feeling the pain of loss more strongly than the joy of gain? Take a moment to express gratitude for the awareness of this psychological insight, helping you make more mindful decisions in the future.

39. Sailing

Self-Reflection: Reflect on the importance of not making assumptions and being non-judgmental in your interactions with others. How has a moment of misjudgment or prejudice affected your perception of someone? What lessons have you learned from such experiences, and how have they influenced the way you approach people and their ambitions? Consider the potential in every individual and the importance of giving them the space to define their own aspirations. Express gratitude for the lessons learned and the opportunity to grow as a more open-minded and empathetic person.

40. Rasam The Magical Recipe

Self-Reflection: How can we integrate traditional dishes like rasam, celebrated for their delightful flavors and health advantages, into our contemporary diets, fortifying our overall well-being and immunity, particularly in light of health challenges such as the COVID-19 pandemic? Let's acknowledge the significance of traditional dishes like rasam with gratitude.

41. Unlove: A Liberation From Limiting Love

Self Reflection: Reflect on the idea of "unloving" as a way to detach from people, places, or habits that limit your growth without fostering hate. Have you ever experienced a situation where unloving, rather than hating, could have helped you move on peacefully? Take a moment to express gratitude for the ability to let go with grace and emotional balance.

42. Matrix Defines Purpose

Self-Reflection: How have the Matrix trilogy's philosophical and metaphysical themes resonated with your understanding of purpose and existence? What aspects of the movies do you appreciate the most and feel grateful for, especially in terms of their impact on your perspective?

43. Attitude Of Being A Custodian

Self-Reflection: How can adopting the perspective of being custodians of our possessions and experiences transform our outlook on life and interactions with others? What positive changes can such a mindset bring, and how can we cultivate a sense of gratitude for this philosophical approach?

44. When Emojis Disrupted The Way We Communicate

Self-Reflection: How has the use of emojis and smileys impacted your digital communication and emotional expression? Do you find them to be effective in conveying emotions in your online interactions? Let's express gratitude for the role emojis play in our digital conversations.

45. Guru Dispels The Darkness Of Ignorance

Self-Reflection: Have you ever had a mentor or guru who played a significant role in shaping your life and guiding you toward your goals? How have their guidance and wisdom influenced your journey? Let's express gratitude and jot down the names of the mentors and gurus who have had a positive impact on our lives.

46. We Can Wait A Minute

Self-Reflection: Have you ever experienced or witnessed a situation where someone was trying to learn something new but faced criticism or impatience from others? How did that experience make you feel, and what did you learn from it? Let's express gratitude for those who have shown kindness and patience to us in our learning endeavors.

47. Legend Of Field Marshal Sam Manekshaw

Self-Reflection: Have you ever been inspired by a great leader's dedication to their duty and country, even in their final moments? How does the story of Field Marshal Sam Manekshaw's unwavering commitment to his duty make you feel, and what lessons can we learn from his life and legacy? Let's express gratitude for leaders like him who have shaped our nation.

48. Goddess Of Grace: A Teacher's Gift On Onam

Self-Reflection: Have you ever experienced an act of kindness or support from a teacher or mentor that made a significant impact on your childhood? How did their gesture influence your feelings and actions at that time? Let's express gratitude for the teachers and mentors who have positively shaped our lives.

49. Niyyah: The Purpose Behind Every Action

Self Reflection: Reflect on the concept of *Niyyah*–the purpose behind your actions and the systems you build in life. Have you ever considered how the clarity of your intentions impacts the outcome of your efforts? Take a moment to evaluate the *Niyyah* behind your current pursuits and express gratitude for the insight that purpose brings to your actions and goals.

50. Musa The Trillionaire: Emperor Of The Salt

Self-Reflection: What do you find most inspiring about historical entrepreneurs like Mansa Musa, who built vast wealth and empires by selling essential consumer goods? How can their success stories influence and motivate modern entrepreneurs in the consumer goods industry? Let's express gratitude for the lessons we can learn from these visionary business leaders.

51. The Power Of Undivided Attention

Self-Reflection: How does the story of Andrew Carnegie's ability to maintain focused attention for extended periods inspire you in your pursuits? What lessons can we learn from his dedication and concentration when it comes to achieving our own goals and dreams? Let's express gratitude for the valuable insights we gain from this story.

52. Parallel Tracks Of Influence: Balancing Forces In History

Self-Reflection: Reflect on the concept of parallel tracks in history and in your own life. Have you encountered situations where opposing or alternative viewpoints played a crucial role in achieving a balanced outcome? How do such parallel tracks contribute to a more well-rounded perspective? With gratitude, you can jot down the names of people who challenge the status quo and bring balance to some larger goals that have influenced you positively.

53. Tamil: Language Of The Heart

Self-Reflection: Reflect on the role language and communication played in this story of helping a fellow traveler in need. Have you ever been in a situation where language barriers created challenges or misunderstandings? How can humbling moments like these inspire gratitude for the ability to bridge gaps and help those in need.

54. Beyond The Physical: Exploring Receptivity

Self-Reflection: Have you ever experienced a connection or resonance with someone's emotions or energies, even when they were far away? Let's express gratitude for our ability to sense and connect with the energies around us.

55. Inclusive Innovation: Lessons From Hong Kong

Self-Reflection: Have you ever been inspired by a place or experience that emphasized inclusivity and accessibility for differently-abled individuals? How can we, as individuals and society, work towards greater inclusivity and tap into the potential of differently abled individuals? Let's express gratitude for those who champion inclusivity and accessibility in various aspects of life.

56. Kuyili: The Immortal Warrior of Sivaganga

Self Reflection: Reflect on the story of Kuyili, the courageous warrior who sacrificed herself for the freedom of her people. How often do we remember and honor the contributions of unsung heroes, especially women and individuals from marginalized communities? Take a moment to express gratitude for their sacrifices, which have profoundly shaped the freedoms and systems we enjoy today.

57. Embracing The Subtle Extraordinarily

Self-Reflection: How often do you pause and engage mindfully with your senses, immersing yourself in the subtle intricacies of touch, taste, smell, sight, and sound while appreciating the rich tapestry of experiences these senses bring into your life? You can gratefully jot down the deep sensory experiences you have noticed made your living experience profound in the physical dimension of your life.

58. Humans Of Tokyo

Self Reflection: Have you ever experienced unexpected acts of kindness that left a lasting impression on you? How can you, in turn, extend such kindness to others in your daily life? Take a moment to express gratitude for the warmth and humanity of strangers who create meaningful connections, even if only for a brief moment.

59. A Sustainable Footwear Revolution

Self-Reflection: How does the story of this footwear startup inspire you to think about creative solutions to global challenges? Let's express gratitude for innovative entrepreneurs who strive to make the world a better place through their initiatives.

60. Sculpting Minimalism: Crafting Beauty In Simplicity

Self-Reflection: How does the concept of minimalism, as shared by the sculptor, resonate with your own life and possessions? Have you ever felt the need to declutter and simplify your life? How can practicing minimalism contribute to your sense of fulfillment and happiness? Let's express gratitude for the idea of minimalism and its potential to bring greater contentment.

61. The Empty Pot: A Seeker's Perspective

Self-Reflection: How does the Zen story about the empty pot and the mindset of a disciple resonate with your own approach to learning and receiving wisdom? Have you ever found it challenging to empty your mind of preconceived notions or prejudices when seeking knowledge or guidance? How can you embrace the concept of an "empty pot" to enhance your learning and personal growth? How grateful are you for this valuable perspective?

62. Shades Of Blue: Comfort And Joy

Self-Reflection: Have you ever noticed a dominant color or pattern in your wardrobe or personal belongings? What do you think this color or pattern says about your personality or preferences? How does the color blue, or any other color you resonate with, make you feel, and what significance does it hold in your life? Let's express gratitude for the colors and patterns that bring us comfort and happiness.

63. The Dance Of Meaningful Coincidences

Self-Reflection: Reflect on the concept of synchronicity and how it relates to your own life experiences. Can you recall moments of meaningful coincidences or events that seemed to align perfectly? Take a moment to express gratitude for the mysterious and serendipitous occurrences that have influenced your journey.

64. Mondo Bongo

Self-Reflection: Can you think of a song or piece of music that holds a special place in your heart and has the power to transport you to joyful moments? Consider taking a moment today to express gratitude to the song and its creators, perhaps by sharing it with a friend or writing a note of appreciation here.

65. You Can Touch Way 'Deeper'

Self-Reflection: After learning about the remarkable human tactile perception mentioned in the story, can you commit to engaging with the world more consciously through your sense of touch, appreciating the intricate details and textures that surround you? Take a moment to consider how you might express gratitude for this remarkable gift that allows you to connect with the physicality of the world and jot it down.

66. Choosing The Five: The Power Of Social Circles

Self-Reflection: After contemplating Jim Rohn's insightful quote about being the average of the five people you spend the most time with, can you evaluate the individuals you engage with most in both your physical and virtual life? How can you make conscious choices about the people you surround yourself with, ensuring they align with your aspirations and values? Take a moment to reflect on ways you can express gratitude for the wisdom this perspective brings to your life.

67. Wabi-Sabi: Embracing Imperfect Perfection

Self-Reflection: After learning about the concept of Wabi-Sabi and its celebration of imperfection and originality, can you take a moment to assess your own life and the societal pressures that may have influenced your pursuit of perfection? How can you embrace the beauty of imperfection, be more content with your genuine self, and express gratitude for the possibility of living an imperfectly perfect life according to the principles of Wabi-Sabi? Jot down your thoughts.

68. Exascale Computing: Revolutionizing Our Technological Landscape

Self-Reflection: After learning about the incredible capabilities of exascale machines and their potential to transform various aspects of our lives, can you take a moment to contemplate the profound impact that advanced technology has on our world? Take a moment to feel grateful for the dedicated scientists and researchers who are pushing the boundaries of what's possible with these machines.

69. It's Not Net Sitting Or Net Eating

Self-Reflection: After hearing the perspective on networking as "NetWorking" rather than "Net Sitting" or "Net Eating," how can you approach your networking efforts with a more proactive and engaged mindset? Take a moment to reflect on how this shift in perspective can enhance your networking experiences, and express gratitude for the valuable insight that can potentially transform your professional connections.

70. Sowing Seeds Of Patience: Lessons From The Farmland

Self-Reflection: How can you apply the valuable lesson of patience to various aspects of your life, whether it's nurturing relationships, cultivating knowledge, or growing wealth? Take a moment to express gratitude for the capacity for sensible patience within you and its role in helping you sow the seeds for the life you desire.

71. Timenomics: Maximizing The Value Of Every Second

Self-Reflection: After reading the insightful analogy of time being akin to 86,400 dollars deposited daily into our life's "time bank," how can you reconsider your approach to managing and investing your precious seconds each day? Take a moment to reflect on how you can make the most of your time and express gratitude for this valuable reminder of the importance of using your time wisely.

72. Dots: Simplifying Success, One Hour At A Time

Self-Reflection: After discovering the "DOTS" philosophy of "Do One Thing Surely," can you identify your own "DOTS" in life, that one thing you can commit to doing for at least an hour daily? How can you incorporate this focused action into your daily routine and trust that it will eventually yield remarkable results? Take a moment to express gratitude for the valuable lesson in singular dedication and the potential it holds for your personal growth and accomplishments.

73. Cracking The Habit Loop: Insights From 'The Power Of Habit'

Self-Reflection: After learning about the habit loop and the idea that we can replace a habit by maintaining the cue and reward while shifting the routine, how can you apply this knowledge to the habits you'd like to change or develop in your life? Take a moment to reflect on how you can use this concept to transform your habits and express gratitude for the valuable insights shared by Charles Duhigg in his book "The Power of Habit."

74. Gut Microbiome: Guardians Of Our Well-Being

Self-Reflection: After reading about the incredible role of the gut microbiome in our overall well-being, can you take a moment to reflect on how you can support and nurture your gut health? How might a balanced gut microbiome impact your emotions, intellect, instincts, and intuition? Express gratitude for the vital role that these trillions of bacteria play in making your life possible, and consider ways to maintain a healthy gut.

75. Tonality: Enhancing Communication Effectiveness

Self-Reflection: After coming across the quote, “Communication is one thing, but your tone of communication is everything,” can you reflect on the significance of tone in your own interactions with others? How might paying attention to your tone improve your communication and relationships? Take a moment to express gratitude for the valuable reminder that effective communication involves not just what you say but how you say it.

76. Spreading Smiles

Self-Reflection: Can you take a moment to reflect on the people who made you smile today and express gratitude for their positive influence on your life? How can you continue to spread smiles and positivity to others as well? Pause and appreciate the simple yet profound act of making someone smile.

77. Transforming Shoulds Into Musts

Self-Reflection: After learning about the distinction between "should" and "must" when it comes to executing tasks and achieving goals, can you reflect on the things in your life that you can elevate from the "should" category to the "must" category? How can this shift in perspective enhance your ability to execute and move closer to your desired destination? Take a moment to express gratitude for the valuable insight that can help you prioritize and achieve your goals more effectively.

78. Memories Framed: Gratitude For Photographs

Self-Reflection: After reflecting on the value of old photographs in preserving memories and taking you on a journey through your past, how can you ensure that you continue to cherish and preserve these precious visual memories? Take a moment to consider the significance of photographs in your life and express gratitude for the ability to relive cherished moments through them.

79. An Angel On The Highway

Self-Reflection: How can you reflect on the idea that some people come into our lives like illusions, fulfill their purpose, and then disappear without seeking acknowledgment or thanks? Is there a moment in your life when you have been that person for someone else, offering assistance without expecting anything in return? Take a moment to express gratitude for the kindness and assistance you received in such magical ways!

80. Discerning Love: What It Is And Isn't

Self-Reflection: After reading about the perspective on what love is not, how can you reflect on your own experiences and understand the true nature of love? Have you encountered any misconceptions about love in your life? Take a moment to express gratitude for the love you have experienced and consider how a clear perspective can help you recognize genuine love in your relationships and life.

81. Leadership In Adversity: Embracing Failure With Responsibility

Self-Reflection: After hearing the story of Dr. APJ Abdul Kalam's experience and the qualities of a leader who embraces failure and takes responsibility, how can you reflect on your own approach to failure and leadership? Have there been instances where you have embraced failure as a learning opportunity and taken responsibility for your actions? Take a moment to express gratitude for leaders who inspire by their qualities, and consider how you can adapt such leadership qualities in your own life.

82. Heartfelt Correction: A Grateful Remembrance

Self-Reflection: Reflect on the importance of constructive feedback and the role it plays in personal and professional growth. Can you recall a time when someone provided you with valuable feedback that helped you improve or correct a mistake? How did their feedback impact you? Take a moment to express gratitude for those who genuinely want you to excel and are brave enough to provide constructive criticism when needed.

83. Seeds Of Devil And Divine

Self-Reflection: Consider the idea that every person has both the potential for goodness and the potential for negativity within them, and it's our actions and interactions that influence which side is nurtured and grows. Reflect on a situation where you consciously chose to nurture the divine aspect in someone, leading to a positive outcome. How can you continue to cultivate the better qualities in those around you? Take a moment to express gratitude for the power within you to inspire positivity in others.

84. Guarding Dignity: Stories Behind The Uniform

Self-Reflection: Take a moment to reflect on the story of the security guard who went from being a successful businessman to working as a security guard due to challenging circumstances. How does this story inspire you to appreciate the people who perform seemingly ordinary tasks in your everyday life, such as security guards, and recognize the extraordinary stories and experiences they may carry with them? Consider expressing your gratitude for their presence and the roles they play in our society.

85. A Cosmic Response

Self-Reflection: Reflect on the moment when two strangers extended their kindness and shared a meal with you during a time of need. Consider how this act of kindness made you feel and the impact it had on your perception of the universe and human nature. Have you ever been in a position to help someone in a similar way? Take a moment to express gratitude for the kindness of strangers and the interconnectedness of humanity.

86. The Journey Vs. Destination

Self-Reflection: Take a moment to reflect on whether you tend to focus more on the journey or the destination in your own life. Consider how this preference has influenced your experiences and decisions. Is there a particular moment or situation where you consciously choose one over the other, and what was the outcome? Express gratitude to the people who helped you understand the significance of both the journey and the destination.

87. For All Unknown Singers

Self-Reflection: Reflect on the dedication and passion of the singer in the story at the restaurant, who continued to perform regardless of the size of the audience or the level of appreciation. Have you ever pursued a passion or profession with a similar level of commitment and detachment from external validation? Take a moment to express gratitude for the artists and performers who bring joy to our lives, often in the background.

88. The Art Of Introspection

Self-Reflection: Reflect on the practice of looking into a mirror as a form of introspection and self-discovery. Have you ever taken the time to truly observe yourself in a mirror, not just for grooming but to understand yourself better? Consider incorporating this practice into your routine and its potential impact on your self-perception and self-liking. Express gratitude for the thought leaders who inspired you to embrace introspection as a valuable tool for self-improvement.

89. The Power Of Follow-Up

Self-Reflection: Reflect on the significance of consistent and persistent follow-up in various aspects of life, including business interactions, personal relationships, and goal achievement. Have you encountered situations where follow-up played a crucial role in achieving success or maintaining relationships? How can the principle of constant, shameless follow-up be applied to improve different facets of your life? Take a moment to express gratitude for the guidance and insights you have received about the importance of follow-up in both professional and personal contexts.

90. Kindness Brewed With Tea

Self Reflection: Reflect on the unexpected kindness shown by the stranger who went out of his way to serve you tea, even though it wasn't his responsibility. Have you ever encountered such acts of kindness from strangers that left you feeling grateful? How can you embrace opportunities to show small acts of kindness to others in your everyday life? Take a moment to express gratitude for the goodness in people, even those we may never meet again.

91. Tale Of Sudhakaran: The Luck Selle

Self-Reflection: Reflect on the story of Sudhakaran, who displayed remarkable honesty and integrity by informing his customer Ashokan about a winning lottery ticket, even though he could have kept it for himself. Have you ever faced a similar situation where your integrity was put to the test? How do you prioritize honesty and righteousness in your own life, even when faced with difficult choices? Take a moment to express gratitude for individuals like Sudhakaran, who inspire us with their moral character.

92. Decisive Whispers: Your Body's Guidance

Self-Reflection: Reflect on the technique described in the story, which involves paying attention to your body's physical responses when faced with decisions. Have you ever used this method or a similar one to make choices? How do you typically approach decision-making, and do you think incorporating bodily cues could be helpful? Take a moment to express gratitude for the valuable techniques and tools that can assist you in making better decisions in life.

93. The Procrastination Puzzle: Unraveling Its Psychology

Self-Reflection: Reflect on your own experiences with procrastination and the insights from the podcast that suggest it happens when we don't truly want to do something. Can you identify areas in your life where you often procrastinate? How can you apply the idea of doing things you genuinely want to do to overcome procrastination and enhance your productivity? Take a moment to express gratitude for the valuable knowledge and perspectives you gain from sources like podcasts, which contribute to your personal growth.

94. Mocha: A Journey From Port To Palate

Self-Reflection: Reflect on the story of Baba Budan and the introduction of coffee to South India. Consider how one person's journey and curiosity led to a significant cultural and economic impact. Are there moments in your life when you've been curious and taken action to explore something new, leading to unexpected outcomes? Take a moment to express gratitude for the individuals like Baba Budan, who have enriched our lives.

95. Transistors: The Invisible Architects Of The Digital Age

Self-Reflection: After learning about the role of transistors in modern computing and their incredible impact on technology, take a moment to reflect on the interconnectedness of our digital world. Consider how these tiny components, each smaller than a strand of hair, power the devices and systems we rely on daily. Are there other aspects of our digital age that you're curious about and would like to explore further? Express gratitude for the brilliant minds behind the remarkable progress in technology that has shaped our lives.

96. The Witness State: Navigating Life's Unfolding Journey

Self-Reflection: Reflect on the concept of 'witnessing' mentioned in the story. Have you ever found yourself unnecessarily engaged in problems or situations around you that didn't necessarily require your involvement? How can you adopt a perspective of Witnessing rather than an immediate response that changes the way you approach the events in and around your life? Take a moment to express gratitude for the perspective shared by Osho Rajneesh.

97. Night Owl Reflections

Self-Reflection: Reflect on your own sleep patterns and the reasons behind them. Are you more inclined to be a night owl or an early bird? Consider the motivations and driving forces that keep you awake or prompt you to wake up early. Are there specific poems, quotes, or pieces of literature that inspire and influence your daily life? Take a moment to express gratitude for the sources of inspiration that shape your routines and habits.

98. Only This Will Lead You To That

Self-Reflection: Reflect on the wisdom contained in Rumi's words: "I asked, 'Why have I received only this?' A voice replied, 'Only this will lead you to That.'" Have you ever experienced moments of uncertainty or difficulty in your life and wondered why you were facing them? How can you apply Rumi's perspective to your own challenges and see them as opportunities for growth and progress? Take a moment to express gratitude for the timeless wisdom of poets and thinkers like Rumi, whose words continue to inspire and guide us.

99. When They Go Low, We Go High

Self-Reflection: Have you ever been in a similar situation where you had to choose between responding negatively or taking the higher road? How can you apply this principle to your own life when faced with challenges or conflicts? Take a moment to express gratitude for the wisdom of responding with grace and dignity, even in difficult circumstances.

100. The Power Of Gratitude

Self-Reflection: Reflect on the power of gratitude and how it can transform your perspective on life. Take a moment to express your gratitude for the gift of life and the power of gratitude itself.

Dedication + Flashback

One midnight during the pandemic, I was alone. I had touched the lowest point in my life. Everything around me felt like it was falling apart. I was lying on a bed when suddenly, I jumped out of it, breathing heavily, trying to regain control.

And in that moment of panic, I started paying attention to my breath.

I realized, yes, I am breathing.

Yes, at least I am able to breathe properly.

And for the first time in a long while, I felt deeply grateful... just for the ability to breathe.

Then, in that dark room, I started seeing hundreds and thousands of things popping up like bubbles around me, things I should be grateful for.

It was a tipping point. A revelation. Something like a Satori moment, a sudden awakening.

And in that stillness, I found myself becoming the most calm and contented being on this planet.

That night, I felt a strong urge to communicate this feeling. I announced on social media that I was going to write something called #365DaysOfGratitude

When I look back now, that moment was the beginning of everything, the beginning of my journey of counting the blessings in my life.

As Steve Jobs once said, "You can't connect the dots looking forward; you can only connect them looking backwards."

Later, I discovered that this simple act of pausing, breathing, and being grateful is a powerful way to regain awareness and restore inner balance. A balanced state of mind, emotion, intellect, and energy becomes the foundation upon which every stone of success is laid.

Today, I dedicate this book to that night... and to all the people, systems, universal forces, and invisible threads that made that moment possible.

About the Author

Amarnath Sankar is an entrepreneur with over a decade of expertise in the media production industry. As the Founder & CEO of CAT Productions®, Amarnath leads a dynamic team that delivers innovative video content solutions to a global clientele. He is also involved in the technology and F&B businesses.

Amarnath is known for his bilingual blog series, #365daysofGratitude, which holds a place in the India Book of Records. This project reflects his resilience and positivity during the Covid-19 pandemic, emphasizing the transformative power of gratitude to inspire and uplift in challenging times.

He holds a degree in Electronics and Communication Engineering and an MBA from the Indian Institute of Management (IIMK), Kozhikode. Amarnath was honored with the Swami Vivekananda Yuva Prathibha Puraskar for Entrepreneurship by the Government of Kerala in 2020. He is also a sought-after keynote speaker at several prestigious colleges and universities.

Amarnath Sankar has authored articles for publications like Business World, New Indian Express, and Mathrubhumi.

Connect with the Author

Scan this QR code to join our Gratitude Circle, unlock exclusive reader bonuses, win assured gifts, and stay in touch!

Includes:

- A free e-book on conscious living
- Access to upcoming events & workshops
- Behind-the-scenes stories from the book
- Links to follow Amarnath on Instagram, LinkedIn, and more

Printed at Repro India Ltd.